LEAVES FROM THE LIFE OF
A COUNTRY DOCTOR

LEAVES FROM THE LIFE OF A COUNTRY DOCTOR

(CLEMENT BRYCE GUNN, M.D., J.P.)

EDITED BY

RUTHERFORD CROCKETT

WITH A FOREWORD BY

JOHN BUCHAN

Birlinn

This edition published in 2002 by
Birlinn Limited
West Newington House
10 Newington Road
Edinburgh
EH9 1QS

www.birlinn.co.uk

First published in 1935 by
TheMoray Press, Edinburgh and London

ISBN 1 84158 238 7

British Library Cataloguing-in-Publication Data
A catalogue record for this book is available from the British Library

Printed and bound by Cox & Wyman Ltd, Reading

FOREWORD

Our Border country has always been noted for its doctors, such as Sir Walter Scott has drawn in his Gideon Gray, men endowed often with high professional skill and always with a stiff sense of duty and a rich humanity. Such in earlier days were Dr Reid of Peebles and Dr Anderson of Selkirk, whose doings have been chronicled by the author of *Rab and his Friends*, the most famous of them all.

The fine tradition is not dead, and I am glad that my old friend, Dr Clement Gunn, has left these reminiscences behind him, for they provide a record of a fast-disappearing Scotland and a picture of a most vigorous, idiomatic and endearing character. I may claim, I think, to have known him from my earliest childhood, for he came to Peebles nearly half-a-century ago and spent there his working life. "I would rather go back to Africa," said Mungo Park, "than practise again in Peebles." Dr Gunn did not find the task penitential. He loved the place and its inhabitants, and drew to himself the affection and respect of a wide country-side. Medicine was his profession, but he had a score of other interests, and he made himself the ecclesiastical historian of the county, producing, in the intervals of a busy career, many valuable antiquarian studies. Few men have led a more full and useful life, and I welcome the story of it because it recalls for me many memories of Tweedside, and above all the figure of an old and much-esteemed friend.

John Buchan.

FOREWORD TO THE BIRLINN EDITION

I was only seven when my grandfather died, so my memories of him are largely second hand. For example, I remember, a few years ago, having my hair cut by a Peebles barber. When I mentioned I was Dr Gunn's grandson, the barber became extremely excited and exclaimed, "You are the Gunner's grandson!" and promptly began telling me stories about him. Indeed I became rather anxious as this was going on while he continued to cut my hair!

This book tells about the life of a remarkable man who was greatly loved and respected for what he did for his town, his county and his people. It also gives a glimpse of what the occupation of a GP was like in the early part of the twentieth century.

I am delighted that Birlinn has decided to reprint the story of his life.

SIR CAMERON RUSBY
YEOVIL
SEPTEMBER 2002

CONTENTS

In the coldest week of the century I first saw the light,
in a corner house in St Patrick Square, Edinburgh,
on 17th December 1860.

My father, George Gunn, assistant editor of *The
Edinburgh Courant*, was then lying sick of what proved
his last illness, which carried him off on the 19th of the
following May (1861), when I was five months old.

My health and constitution were excessively delicate,
so that no hopes of my survival were encouraged. But,
despite the rigorous winter, three things pulled me
through:—the grace of God; a mother's love; and
sack whey.

My mother was widowed at the age of thirty-three,
my father being thirty-six years old when he died,
leaving her with six children between the ages of ten
years and five months.

Shortly after her widowhood a flitting became
necessary, and my mother removed to N.W. Circus
Place.

Here, by a peculiar but quite agreeable arrangement,
we acquired, in addition to the usual fixtures, a human
accessory in the shape of the Rev. Dr Veitch, a Greek
scholar of considerable reputation. At this time he was
engaged on his *magnum opus*, a volume on Greek Verbs,
irregular and defective. The floor of his sitting-room
was completely covered with books; two lanes of
carpet led to the two doorways. At nights, this *savant*
entertained many visitors of literary and journalistic
distinction, among them Russel of *The Scotsman*, Pat
Alexander, and others, toddy in rummers being always

9

indulged in at these symposia. On his receiving the degree of LL.D. from the University of Edinburgh, Dr Veitch's friends presented him with his portrait, which was hung above our dining-room fireplace. It now hangs in the Scottish Portrait Gallery in Edinburgh.

At Circus Place, then, we lived from about 1865 till 1882, when my mother gave up housekeeping. Her fourth child, a boy, had died at an early age, so the family now numbered five; four sons and a daughter.

With most of the neighbouring children, including the Littlejohns round in the Circus, we played in the Gardens opposite, or attempted cricket of a sort in what was then known as "John Hope's Park," in Stockbridge, now all built over.

The drawing-room of the house looked to the north, away over the Firth of Forth, with the revolving light of Inchkeith Lighthouse right in front of its windows. To the west, in the far distance, we could descry the Grampian Hills, with Ben Ledi and other peaks outlined against the horizon on summer evenings.

My mother continued through the years to keep her connection with Lady Yester's Parish Church, of which the Rev. Dr Gray was minister. He had married my parents, and had baptized all their children. Twice each Sunday we were escorted from Circus Place up Hanover Street across Princes Street, then up the steep Mound, along George IV. Bridge and College Street to the church. In the afternoons it was a terrible race; and the "merry" pealing of the bells of St Andrew's Church in George Street always caused a feeling of sickness in me as we hurried upward and onward. The family returned homeward after service, but I had to remain for Sunday school, and trudged slowly downhill at five o'clock.

Dr Gray was the model family minister and pastor, who knew the Christian name of every child in his flock. A little boy was dying, and being tremulous, asked his father at the bedside: "Will Dr Gray be there in heaven, Father?" "Yes," replied he. "Then," said his little son, "I don't mind dying." This affords some idea of the hold that this good man had on children. When he used to visit us, he would cause me to climb on his knee and search among his dark curly hair for threepenny-bits, which he permitted me to retrieve with triumph in the end.

At the age of five I entered on school life. St Stephen's School was the arena.

This school, yet in existence, a large substantial building in St Stephen's Street (then called Brunswick Street), was surmounted by a huge open Bible wrought in stone, the first piece of sculpture executed by the artist who later became Sir John Steel, but was then a young lad. The senior girls were situated on the top floor; the senior boys in the middle; and we "infants" on the street floor. I got on famously for a time, but in the end disgraced myself in the following manner.

Having attained the top row in our room, as dux boy I occupied the seat next that of the dux girl. She was a lovely child; I can see her yet. Her features were regular and beautiful; her skin pure and fair; finely moulded and dimpled arms lay upon her white pinafore; long fair ringlets curled round her neck and fell upon her shoulders. At the close of each session, forenoon and afternoon, we were wont to stand with hands closed in front of our faces, and to repeat the Lord's Prayer. Alas, one day, in the very middle of the prayer, human nature could hold out no longer; *I kissed her!*

She uttered a squeal and sank down, burying her blushing face in her hands. At that very moment, the preceptress, who had been praying with open eyes, howled out: *"Clement Gunn has kissed A—— K——!"* The whole school turned about and gazed in awed wonder at the infant Don Juan. I was marched out forthwith, and forbidden to return in the afternoon.

My mother was duly told all about her youngest's villainy; she laughed heartily; and all was over. I returned to school next day. But the Fair One remained away for a week, and would not speak to me ever again. I have never seen her since. We were both aged about six. But there were giants in the earth in those days!

In 1869, when a little over the age of eight, I entered Heriot's Hospital as a boarding scholar. Two of my elder brothers had been educated there, and when my time came in turn, Peter, who was some eighteen months older than I, was still at school, and was of some comfort to me, though Tom had left.

To my dear mother the parting with her Benjamin was a terrible wrench; to me it was heart-rending.

My new schoolfellows were strong and rough; I was delicate and gently nurtured. I was homesick continually. All the masters, save one, were severe; some were brutal. The visiting masters (for writing, singing, drawing, French, and dancing) were all unmercifully teased by the boys, and suffered much. Their sufferings were, however, amply avenged upon the boys by the resident staff.

In spite of all this, we were well educated and thoroughly grounded in the essentials or institutes of a sound education. Our memories were cultivated by repetition only, as *thinking* was not thought of in those days! To this very hour I can repeat every date in history, and every question in the Shorter Catechism.

My health too greatly improved during those six years in Heriot's. Hitherto I had been so delicate as not to be expected to live.

Later, when a spell of ill-health supervened and I was sent home, a physician of the cold-blooded school handled me like a dying kitten and sneered: "However did *you* get into Heriot's?"

My entrance there had indeed been a narrow shave!

With that exception I had no illnesses; and so it was with the other boys; life at school in the open air was healthy, bracing us up, and increasing our resistance to illness of all kinds.

But I was nervous from birth, as both my parents were in bad health when I was conceived and born.

The rigorous treatment of the masters at school greatly aggravated this tendency, which continues to this day, though I do my best that it be not shown. And this nervousness, coupled with an unfortunately vivid imagination, has caused me lifelong continuing wretchedness; I must ever expect the worst, which does not come!

One pleasant feature marked our walks home from school on Saturdays—namely, patting on the back dear "Greyfriars Bobby." This faithful, great-hearted terrier watched by his master's grave, near Greyfriars gate, for many years, leaving it only when the one-o'clock gun fired, which was his signal to trot into Mr Trail's eating-house hard by, for his soup and plateful of bones. The Baroness Burdett-Coutts afterwards erected a monument in bronze to this loyal four-footed friend at the top of Candlemaker Row.

From Heriot's, too, we had an excursion annually to Kinross, Peebles, Selkirk, Kelso, St Andrews, and elsewhere, by which means we got to know Scotland in a small degree. I little thought, on that pouring wet day at Peebles in 1871, that one day I would be a doctor there, and church historian!

After a period of six years at Heriot's I left in 1875, being "the most meritorious of the youths completing their education" at that particular time, and on that account obtaining the medal. I obtained also a bursary of thirty pounds for five years wherewith to pay my expenses at the University, but for the next eighteen months would be a "Hopeful Scholar," living at home, and pursuing the special subjects for the preliminary examinations for Medicine, under the Heriot's masters.

Well do I remember the terrors of the inquisition in the council-room of the Hospital, before the Lord Provost and magistrates and clergy of the city. "Well, Gunn, what do you intend to be?" inquired the Lord Provost. "Please, sir, an editor," said I. A burst of laughter, and a gentle smile from Dr Bedford, welcomed my reply. "Why do you want to be that?" "Because my father was," said I. "Well, you can't be that, you had better be a minister." "No, I'm not good enough; if I can't be an editor, I'll be a doctor." I then still had the idea, in which we had all been trained at home, that ministers were saints above all men.

When I told my mother of my decision, she remarked with wise prescience: "You have chosen a most toilsome profession, but we will all help you as much as possible, although the expense is very great." She was right in both particulars.

At this crisis in my youth the family stood thus: I, the youngest, was aged fourteen, about to study for the Medical Preliminary. Peter, eighteen months older, was attending the University for his M.A. degree, and taking private teaching at nights with Academy boys. Tom, next above him, was a law clerk with Mr Walls, S.S.C., in Heriot Row. George, the eldest, was secretary in the office of Messrs Renton & Gray, in George Street, taking classes also at the University for his M.A. degree. He and Peter were intended for the Church.

George was allowed away for a few hours during the day to attend his classes, but had to return to the office at night until nine o'clock—a hard life. My sister Margaret was at this time living at home. Our mother presided over all, taking an interest in each of our varied subjects; stimulating us, guiding us, managing the house, and acting as sole treasurer of all the funds contributed by each member of the family. It was a real and true communism.

There were at that time seven compulsory subjects for the Medical Preliminary Examinations: English, Arithmetic, Mathematics, Latin, French, Logic, and Mechanics. Greek was optional, but the degree of Doctor of Medicine could not be taken without it. Many candidates placated themselves with the intention of studying Greek during their University course, "any time before graduation," and thereafter found it impossible to do so. I was informed that I should not be permitted to matriculate until I had passed in all the subjects, including Greek, before entering the University.

I entered for six of the subjects at the earliest opportunity, and passed in all; reserving Logic and Mechanics, which were new to me, till the last, when I passed in these also.

In connection with those eight subjects an extraordinary thing occurred, which puzzles me to this day. I had a capital memory, but no brain for mathematics. To this hour I do not understand *why* "the square of *a* plus *b* equals *a* square, plus two *ab*, plus *b* square." But I committed it to memory, with the whole of Kelland's *Book of Mathematics* and six books of Euclid, the diagrams in which I could visualize with all their original letters of the alphabet.

My master, Henry Smith, had little hope of my passing. I had none. When the results were at length announced, I rushed up to the mathematical-room at the top of the stair, with its oaken roof whereon cannon had formerly been supported, and presented my certificate to Mr Smith. "Well," said he, with a dubious smile, "I suppose you haven't passed?"

"Yes, sir," said I, handing him the certificate. He gave a yell of surprise, mingled with joy. "Mathematics passed *with distinction*!" There it was beyond cavil; I had done the papers, and done the examiners too! This feat cannot now be performed, as instead of setting propositions from Euclid they set deductions, etc., in relation to the propositions. However, I was "through," and that was all that mattered. In Greek also I won through, thus opening the way to a future M.D. degree.

No doubt, however, Henry Smith wondered till his last hour (and at times, even yet, I myself wonder also), "*Was there some mistake?*"

The path to the University was now open, and in 1876, a month before I was sixteen, I matriculated, and took out tickets for Anatomy, Chemistry, and Dissecting.

The University authorities wisely advised candidates to begin their courses in the summer session, but I could not afford to lose six months, so perforce had to begin the study of medicine among the horrors of the dissecting-room.

The buildings were those of the Old University in the South Bridge; the professors were, for Chemistry, Crum Brown (a brother of Dr Brown, author of *Rab and his Friends*); for Anatomy, Turner, who later became Principal. Daniel Cunningham, who afterwards succeeded him in the Anatomy Chair, was senior demonstrator in the dissecting-rooms. Turner was an Englishman, born in Lancaster. There existed for many years in that town two houses on each of which had been erected a tablet recording the extraordinary fact that Principal Sir William Turner was born there! He was a splendid lecturer, without much trace of English dialect, having also complete control of his class. Two jokes only did he permit himself annually to make: "In the hip-joint there is a ligament called the 'Y-shaped' ligament, though *why* it is so called no one knows." The other was by way of a conundrum. When describing the groove in the ulna in which the

16

ulnar nerve runs, he would mention that popularly its name was "the funny-bone; no doubt because it was next to the humerus."

After passing the examination on the Bones in due course, a "part" was allocated to me in the dissecting-room. My "part" was a human arm to be dissected. My companion was an Englishman, by name Richards; and here Dan Cunningham the demonstrator played us a sorry trick. Instead of giving two tyros a well-preserved limb which could be easily dissected, he gave us a "part" (for which we had to pay, I think, seven-and-sixpence each) which was absolutely rotten, practically falling to pieces. It was impossible to learn anything from such a condition of things, but we did what we could, and tried to glean as much as possible from Turner's dissections in the class. I never could afford either to have a second course, as was customary, or to dissect each part of the body twice.

In the summer session, which began in May, the classes were Botany, Zoology, and Practical Chemistry. We attended old Balfour in the Botanical Gardens at eight every morning, a friend and I walking down to Granton Breakwater beforehand, for a bathe in the sea.

For Zoology we had Sir Wyville Thomson, of the *Challenger*, who made the class as interesting as he could. We studied the specimens in the Royal Scottish Museum, then known as the Museum of Science and Art.

My chief chum then, and to the end, was Hugh Sutherland, from Brora, who shared in the matutinal sea-bathing. He belonged to such a stern Free Kirk Sabbatarian family that he even had to shave on Saturday nights instead of on Sundays; this discipline, however, did not prevent him from being very fond of the lasses.

Another very dear chum of University days was

William Thyne, with whom I often walked home at nights. We "did our Bones" together at his house or at ours, and puzzled each other with those of the carpus and tarsus. He kept his in a tub, in a strong solution of washing soda, and on very frosty nights we often had to dig them out with an axe, as they were frozen into one mass in the solution.

In 1878 I went up for, and passed in, the subjects of the First Professional: Botany, Chemistry, Practical Chemistry, and Natural History. This was the first step gained. This examination, like the Preliminary, had the effect of weeding out those who found themselves unfitted intellectually or temperamentally for further study; for myself, the Botany class gave me a "scunner" at the subject which has lasted ever since. Professor Balfour, a very kindly man, was well named "Woody Fibre," as his teaching of what might have been a most interesting subject was of a singularly wooden and fibrous nature.

In my leisure time, such as it was, I now began to take private pupils and to teach in a school. The school was situated in Picardy Place, and was one of those semi-private establishments which were successful until extinguished and superseded by those of the Merchant Company and others. The pupils, of both sexes, hailed chiefly from Leith, and were, the girls especially, boisterous and not very refined. They were all older than I, and exempted from corporal punishment. The result was that one had to endeavour to subdue them by the power of personality. This might have succeeded with boys; the girls simply laughed and made fun of one, not openly, but in a cunning, apparently ingenuous way, not easily detected, and best ignored, as punishment of any kind was impossible.

The result was that being, as I have said, of a nervous temperament, I lived in constant dread of those buxom Leith girls. This, however, was not, I hoped, evident to them, being concealed by a stern official manner.

As school was dismissed at two o'clock, and I had to be at my class in the University at that same hour, I had daily a terrible and sickening rush along Leith Street and up the North and South Bridges, arriving twenty minutes late; the cause of which I explained to the Professor. Then at night came the awful hurry round our pupils, from six till nine; and attempts at study after that.

My brother Peter, with his University textbooks, fingers in ears, would be cramming away in one corner of the study, while Tom at the fireside hammered away at his engineering, his great ambition being to make the smallest possible steam locomotive, which would actually go. In this he succeeded again and again. Between times, he studied German, Natural Philosophy, Livy and other Latin authors, with the intention of being called to the Bar; which ambition we all considered hopeless. At school he had been too much of a fighter to study; hence he could not go to College. He now sought to repair this neglect, and, as it was not possible to become M.A., had resolved to try for the Bar by the side entrance, that of private study.

This was a brave and plucky endeavour, laughed at by all of us; but he plodded on year after year, studying and hammering alternately every night. In the end he did succeed, and was duly called.

I myself would appear on the scene at nine o'clock or later, and sit down to pore over Quain's *Anatomy*. Often I would fall asleep from weariness, but would rise early in the morning to try again when fresh.

We had, of course, at times interesting experiences with our various pupils. At Henderson's Preparatory School in India Street there was a little boy named John Goodeve Miller Erskine. But whenever his name was read aloud as "Erskine," at roll-call, he refused to answer, and when challenged by Mr Henderson would reply: "My name is Lord Garioch." This brought him many a thrashing, but he continued to make his protest notwithstanding.

During those years also, when an Election of Scottish Representative Peers was being announced, whenever the Lord Clerk Register called out the name of the Earl of Mar, an individual among the public always replied: "*Here.*" In his case, the result always was expulsion. This too continued for a while. But in process of time, this man, whose name also was John Goodeve Miller Erskine, made good his claim to the ancient Earldom of Mar, then held by the Earl of Kellie, and he became Earl of Mar of the older creation. And my pupil became in reality Lord Garioch, as he was eldest son of the Earl of Mar. The old Earl is now dead, but in this present year of grace (1929) my wife and I attended the Election of Peers in Holyroodhouse, and there I saw and heard my former pupil answer to his name as Earl of Mar when the roll was called by the Duke of Buccleuch!

During this period I frequently saw Robert Louis Stevenson, as he and his parents sat in St Stephen's Church, and passed our pew every Sunday. We boys called him "The Pirate," because of his lanky black hair, hectic cheek-bones, and bizarre velvet jacket. But he was then quite unknown, nor did we at the time so much as know his name. I was then teaching two Academy boys—sons of a Mr Cunningham living in Ainslie Place. I used to feel annoyed when the library door would open during our lesson, and this dark lanky stranger would walk in. With scant apology he would approach my pupils at the table, and proceed to arrange with them the details of some theatricals about to take place in the private theatre of Professor Fleeming Jenkin.

My pupils then told me who he was; but at that time

he was considered an idle dilettante, though even then he must have produced some of his early works. Later, my brother George used to accompany him down from Masson's class at the University in the afternoons, Stevenson breaking off at Heriot Row.

An amusing incident occurred many years later in connection with one of the two Cunningham boys above-mentioned, my lessons with whom were summarily interrupted by R.L.S.

One day, years afterwards, the Lord Provost and magistrates of Edinburgh lunched at Peebles Hydropathic, and I was invited as a guest. There was one other guest there, who replied for us both to the toast of "The Guests." Thereafter, as we walked down the avenue together, I asked him : "When at the Academy, who was your tutor?" He replied : "A young fellow called Gunn." "That was me," said I, with more truth than grammar. "See what you have produced," he retorted. This was Miller Cunningham of Leithen Lodge, my former pupil. He told me also that his brother, my younger pupil, now "Sir George," was a barrister in London.

I had other pupils as far away as Glengyle Terrace, and even in Caledonian Road, to whom I had to run, or rather rush, nightly; no cars then nor bicycles. In those benighted days we had to foot it every bit of the way, and also to the University every morning, and back in the late afternoon.

No study of any kind was allowed at home on Sundays, which were very strictly observed. We had few companions apart from those at College, but we kept together and invariably went everywhere in a body. As for society, we had little; there was no time, even had there been inclination for it, so that when at last, after years of perpetual grinding at hard study, we were launched forth upon the world, we knew singularly little of its ways.

It was now spring, 1879. Pathology, Physiology, and Materia Medica were the subjects to be attended in classes for the Second Professional Examination; with Anatomy constantly being revised and kept up to standard. I kept the carpus and tarsus bones on strings in my pockets, and in season and out of season pulled these forth and studied them from every possible angle. I possess yet the three beautiful bones of the inner ear (the malleus, incus, and stapes), dissected by myself. In fact, I always smuggled out my bones after dissection, under my coat, and boiled them on the fire at home; then bleached them white for study. Bones from a certain neighbouring churchyard were also, I fear, utilized by some students for purposes of research.

The Professors at this time were, for Pathology, good old Sanders; for Materia Medica, Fraser; and for Physiology, Rutherford. This last was a man of huge dimensions, possessing an Assyrian beard and a magnificent singing voice, of which he was inordinately proud.

I cannot say that these arduous years were altogether happy. We were too hard-wrought in the struggle for education, and had too few chances of distraction or recreation. But there was no time to think about things; we had but to plod on.

Our widowed mother was upheld, during these difficult years, by two considerations. She believed whole-heartedly in the value of prayer, and confided all her desires and disappointments in daily, even in hourly, intercession.

Also she possessed the conviction that she was assisted, all her life long, by the influence of her husband ever with her, supporting and guiding her steps. These two beliefs carried her onwards through her life here, to the very end. Without them she never would have won through with the upbringing of her "big sma' family," amid all her worries, griefs, anxieties, disappointments, and sorrows.

The memory of my father was ever a fine incentive to effort on his children's part; for during his short life of thirty-six years his tireless devotion to duty was recognized by all who knew him, as the most salient peak in his character.

Commenting on his premature death, *The Edinburgh Courant*, with which he had been connected for twenty years, and of which he had been assistant editor for ten, referred (20th May 1861) to one special *tour de force* of his, which in modern journalistic phrase would be known as a " scoop " of the first magnitude. This was "that brilliant and picturesque description of the Volunteer Review of 7th August (1860) which, with surprising rapidity, he committed to writing after witnessing that memorable scene, and which appeared in an evening edition of this Journal *on the same day*."

On his death, those in the journalistic world realized that, as the eminent Hugh Miller said of him, "the never-ending toil and anxiety of newspaper life, which has no Sabbaths in its year, sapped his naturally robust and powerful constitution, and at last prostrated the entire system, even at his early age." His ever-active kindness of heart was reflected in the fact that whenever a former Edinburgh journalist who had gone to Fleet Street wanted a helpful hint on any subject the invariable suggestion was—" *Write to Gunn* "; and the reply was as certain as it was comprehensive.

Fortified by her husband's memory, our mother would never, during all these years of striving, consider defeat. By example, precept, command, and courage she heartened, strengthened, and impelled us each and all to persevere, until at length achievement should be won.

Now occurred an adventurous episode in my life: I
became a locum tenens. For some considerable time
I had attended daily the Royal Infirmary, and had
diligently walked the wards, reading up cases as well as
I knew how.

One day a family friend informed us that his doctor
had never had a holiday, and had asked him to inquire
about a possible locum tenens, so as to permit of his
getting away. Our friend persuaded me to undertake
the duties. I had not passed my Second Professional;
but in those days unqualified assistants were allowed,
and indeed were very common. So away I went,
resplendent in tile hat and surtout, but very homesick
and trembling with nervousness withal. I had never
even travelled before, yet now I was on my way to
England, alone and inexperienced; moreover to live
and act as the sole doctor in a lonely district of Northumberland, miles away from any other practitioner.

A former schoolfellow, when he heard of my enter-
prise, presented me with a small volume which some
medical student friend had apparently discarded.
This was Swayne's *Maxims in Midwifery*. The first line
is burned into my brain to this day. It ran thus:
"When called to a case of midwifery, obey the call at
once: if too soon you can go away; if too late it is not
your fault." This was my sole obstetric equipment!

So off went the doctor, and I sat in his place. One
thing I resolved to do, and that was to leave things alone
and allow Nature to do her own work; I would not if
possible injure anyone actively, though passively this
might occur. I had never seen a maternity case. Now

they began to come in. The messenger always waited on me during the night, and escorted me to the house of doom. There I squatted on a chair by the bedside and gave Nature her chance. This occurred again and again without mishap, until one night I received my shock and punishment. Something went wrong with a young wife of about eighteen, which I "jaloused" was beyond me. So off I sent the young husband to the nearest medical man, nine miles away. What blessed relief when an hour or two thereafter I heard the returning hoofs of his horse! In he came, diagnosed what was wrong, put it right, while I administered the anæsthetic; gave me a few words with a pleasant smile, and was off. He neither let me down, or made any unpleasant remarks; but departed like an angel of light, or rather, of the night. To this day I gratefully remember this man and his great kindness to a raw youth; only about two years ago I observed in the newspapers his death at an advanced age. From him I learned how to treat a young practitioner; to be gentle, long-suffering, and helpful.

My next shock was a surgical one. On a certain Sunday morning a carriage-and-pair drew up in front of the dining-room window, to my great alarm. In walked a stout old fellow in tile hat and surtout, accompanied by his wife. He said never a word; but his mouth remained wide open. The wife also sat down breathless and speechless! What was I to do? I had hastily donned my long coat on recognizing their arrival. I rushed to the bookcase next door, took out Druitt's *Surgeon's Vade Mecum*, and turned up *JAW*. There it was: "Dislocation and its treatment." Adopting my most imposing manner, and now somewhat reassured, I re-entered with both thumbs wrapped up in clean napkins, backed my patient into a strong armchair with a high back, and inserting both thumbs into his mouth pressed hard down on his back molars,

25

slightly raising the chin at the same time. O blessed sound, in went the jaw with a loud click, the napkins shielding my thumbs from a good bite! And away they drove, back again to Haggerston Castle, whence they had come.

Every alternate day I had to ride across the sands for three miles, to Holy Island: I who had never ridden before in my life! Fortunately the steady old white horse never gave any trouble, either from shying or from stumbling. The tides had to be studied, so that one might cross with the falling tide, and return in advance of the rising one. In those days the wooden poles which marked the course across the sands were sparse and far apart, and when the mists descended were frequently obscured, so that one might easily lose the way and be drowned, as had happened at times to others. But my old horse knew the route, and never wandered, even during the night. The first thing I did was always to go to the inn and have a fortifying ham-and-egg tea, for I was ravenous after the journey through the North Sea. I then visited the islanders on foot. In those days Holy Isle was not the fashionable place it has since become; the population consisted of fishers, smugglers, and a few agriculturists. The Castle had not then been restored, but was used as the Coast-guard Station, whose officers had to be attended by me. When time permitted, or when the tide was unsuitable for returning, there was the Abbey for me to visit, and the shore to be minutely dredged for the small encrinites called St Cuthbert's Beads. I collected quite a string of these, which in time were contributed to my younger son's museum.

Patients at Branksome Cottages (on the mainland), around which lies the Field of Flodden, had to be visited at times; and here might be seen a few calthorps, rowels, spearheads, etc., gathered from the soil. From the battlements of Ford Castle, near by, I could see in the far distance the manse of Stichill, in Berwickshire, where my eldest brother now lived as parish minister. This allayed my homesickness a little.

To an older man, and one more experienced, a sojourn in that beautiful part of the English Borders would have been very pleasant and full of interest; but to me, living in an ignorant condition of nervous terror, it was a place of unrest and of unknown happenings. Not that my state of mind was ever, I trust, evident; quite the reverse. I adopted a steady, slow method of speech and manner to conceal my youthful qualms, and to give myself time to recover poise.

Thus my first period of probation came to an end without any untoward accidents or deaths, and the resident doctor returned from his holiday quite pleased. In those days the fee for an unqualified locum tenens was three guineas a week, which I duly received, together with a flattering testimonial, and remitted to my mother.

Undeterred by these experiences in the realms of medicine, surgery, and maternity, I now ventured still further. While still officiating in my first post I was approached by another neighbouring doctor who asked me to become his locum tenens for a time, as he too had not had a holiday for years. Reluctantly I consented, and was thus embarked on further experiences.

My most vivid recollection of this my second professional post is as follows:—

One dark, misty night, when riding along unknown roads, I suddenly found my horse up against a railway gate, with rails underfoot. Dismounting to open the gate, I found some difficulty in doing so, being cumbered with the reins. Suddenly a terrific roar and fearsome rumbling indicated to my strained hearing that the night express was upon us. Redoubling my efforts with the horse, I barely won through the gate when the express dashed by—a narrow squeak indeed. Out rushed the station-master in great alarm, having remembered that the gates were not in order, the first one having been left open across the public road, and the other, which had debarred me, being closed across the rails, thus permitting horse and rider to risk their lives upon the railway track in the murky darkness of the night. The station-master besought me to say nothing about the episode.

One of my patients at Bamburgh was Thomasin Darling, an old woman of about eighty-four, sister of the famous Grace Darling, whose recumbent effigy then lay under a canopy in the churchyard, but has since been removed into the church.

During this time I had a good many more maternity cases, but these gradually came to terrify me less. One of these patients was the wife of the station-master aforesaid, who frequently discussed my narrow escape on the railroad with feelings of relief.

When the resident doctor returned, refreshed, he expressed satisfaction with the manner in which I had gained the confidence of his patients; also with my professional qualifications, which he must have viewed with the eye of faith.

Shortly after this, yet another neighbouring doctor asked me to become his locum tenens, as he, too, badly needed a holiday.

This time I paid the penalty of consent. To his home —a colliery district in Northumberland—I went, though with many misgivings. This was then the largest colliery for steam-coal in the kingdom, well conducted and of up-to-date construction. There was at that time but one doctor in the place.

No sooner had the resident doctor departed and left me alone than my troubles began. An epidemic of malignant scarlet fever broke out in the miners' homes, causing widespread devastation. Whole families were prostrated. There were no nurses then, and no hospital for infectious diseases; nor was there compulsory notification. Miners would go down the pits in the morning, and on coming up at night, find one or more of their children dead. The virus usually attacked the throat. From beneath many of the beds, too, could be heard the heavy breathing and snoring of greyhound dogs; these sounds, with accompanying scents, ascended to the suffering children above. To some of the miners, their dogs were as dear as, or dearer than, their children.

Night and day I perambulated those dwellings; there was little or no country work. I scarcely ever undressed; and at length became exhausted. This was a fearful time. At last, a day or two before the local doctor was due to return, the infection caught me. The throat showed a diphtheritic condition, and the body was sore all over.

The doctor, on his return, wished me to stay and receive attention, but I resolved to go away ere worse trouble developed. So, in great suffering and much weakness of body, I boarded the train for Kelso, and thence crawled rather than walked up the four-mile brae to Stichill Manse. There I went straight to bed, and remained ill for some weeks. My brother George, now minister of Stichill, had made his beautiful manse our other home, surrounding us with all the love and hospitality that his large heart could pour out.

But the winter session at the University was due to begin in November, and through this illness I lost the whole term, and the companionship of the men of my own year.

My eldest brother had previously been for some time assistant minister in St Stephen's, Edinburgh, before his ordination in 1878. At that time St Stephen's was the most fashionable church in Edinburgh, numbering among its members many of the judges and of the aristocracy, with most of the principal medical men of the city.

When my brother became a candidate for the appointment there were other licentiates of his year who coveted this desirable post. So, because our family were members of the church, it was judged advisable that he should preach not once, as did those others, but twice, to ensure absolute impartiality in the appointment. Well do I remember the text of his first sermon after Licence, preached in the now demolished St David's Church: "The Word of the Lord standeth sure, having this sign: The Lord knoweth them that are his." My mother and all of us sat as solitary units, scattered in obscure corners throughout the church and under the gallery, so as not to be seen and thus render the preacher nervous. It was indeed a solemn day for our mother, who now at long last saw the fruition of her hopes and prayers, and her eldest son in the pulpit preaching the Word of God. We all greatly feared and trembled.

My brother George was the most selfless man I ever knew; ever thinking and doing for others. He was devoted to duty, methodical and energetic; with a rare humility, quite devoid of self-consciousness. It was, I believe, his transparent sincerity that throughout his life won and kept the hearts of those who knew him.

The manse of Stichill is one of the most attractively situated in Scotland, about four miles from Kelso, facing the sun to the south and commanding fine views over the whole of the Merse and Teviotdale as far as Berwick, and into Northumberland. In this beautiful and beloved place, then, I had my illness and enjoyed my convalescence.

One of my convalescent activities was a choir screen of Gothic design, with the motto, *Gloria in excelsis Deo*, for use in the church, where an organ (a signal innovation!) had just been installed. This screen I myself designed, carved, and wrought in oak, as a thank-offering for my recovery.

I also accompanied the minister on his three-mile walks to Hume, which, with Stichill, was his joint parish, and we enjoyed sweet converse together, I learning many things from his wide experience and native shrewdness. He was the most faithful minister I have known, devoted to his people, visiting them assiduously however distant; keeping in touch with the youths and maidens after these had left his parish; assisting the old folks with money, advice, and necessaries. Science and Art classes were then being established throughout Scotland, so as a neighbouring schoolmaster was not qualified to teach the required subjects, and earn the grant for his school, my brother undertook to go there regularly to teach. He thus brought on and helped forward many promising youths who in later life obtained important posts as schoolmasters and in other capacities.

The venerable Rev. David Cairns [1] was then minister of the United Presbyterian Church in Stichill. In the time of my brother's predecessor, there had been no comings and goings between the two manses; but this was now altered. My brother and Mr Cairns inaugurated a conjoint Sunday school, taught by the teachers of both churches; also Sunday evening services in each church alternately, conducted by the Parish minister in the U.P. Church, and by the U.P. minister in the Parish Church. This arrangement worked successfully for many years. At that date, when the two denominations were so markedly "by schisms rent asunder," such an example of true Christian unity was rare indeed.

The inhabitants of this Border parish were kindly and hospitable, and we formed many pleasant friendships

[1] Brother of the late Principal, and father of Principal Cairns (Aberdeen) [Ed.].

with those of all conditions. I recollect one story of a farmer who was also a leading elder in a country kirk, and who presented a clock for the front of the kirk gallery. This clock showed some irregularities in striking and time-keeping; its donor also was suspected of irregularities as to *meum* and *tuum*, especially in the matter of other people's sheep, which frequently found their way into his flocks. "Nae wonder," said a shrewd neighbour, "that his kirk clock wunna gang, wi' the lamb's lugs stickin' oot ahint!"

As I grew stronger, we sometimes played lawn-tennis, which was then coming in, at the manse of Ednam. This manse has the good fortune to be the subject of the most ancient Church Charter known, whereby Thor the Long gifted to the parish of Ednam a church and glebe. Recently, in digging a grave along the south wall of Ednam Church, workmen discovered a stone coffin of quite exceptional length; this ancient resting-place may have been that of Thor Longus himself!

Being town-bred boys, we knew nothing of agriculture, and now that we were located in a purely pastoral parish our ignorance became manifest. But my brother, with his intense love of knowledge and his persevering spirit, learned from everyone around him, and in course of time became an authority on gardening, geology, and botany, and on the history and archæology of his parish. He afterwards became President of the Berwickshire Naturalists' Club.

Meanwhile I was grinding away in every spare minute at Anatomy, a subject which I hated, but knew was essential to my future career.

Thus, during these recuperative months, I gathered strength, and became ready for the impending labours of the winter session, 1880-1881.

Among those at College during these years, whom I often saw, were James Barrie, who had just published *An Edinburgh Eleven*; Arthur Conan Doyle, who sat near me in all the classes; and S. R. Crockett, then a tall buirdly Arts student going in for his M.A. The latter was frequently occupied during the lectures in scribbling original verses, undetected by the professors, but not unobserved by his fellow-students. He worked also with other Free Church students at their Mission in St Mary Street, where "Cleg Kelly" dwelt.

My brother Peter and I were then working as members of the University Missionary Association, in Blackfriars Street, reviving and restoring the Old Kirk parish. Our eldest brother had induced us to join this Association, where we took part in Penny Readings on Saturday nights; taught in the Sunday school in the Masons' Hall on Sundays, and diligently visited and hunted up all absentees.

There was then also a weekly Literary Society in connection with St Stephen's Church. In one of our debates, "Is Vivisection justifiable?" in which the affirmative was led off by me, I defeated Christopher Johnstone, afterwards Lord Sands, the distinguished Scottish judge.

In those days the Royal Infirmary was established in the old buildings in Infirmary Street, where the public baths now stand. From Walker and Argyll Robertson, the two oculists of the period, I received the appointment of non-resident house surgeon of the eye ward.

On the first Sunday after term ended I strolled along to see what was going on. A man entered, in shirt, trousers, and slippers, and jumped lightly on the table to have a sarcoma of the orbit removed. He had just taken a few whiffs of the chloroform from the napkin when, with a gasp or two, he died. We all, including the surgeon about to operate, got a terrible gliff. The anæsthetist was in no way to blame, but I had a lucky escape, as had the tragedy occurred a few days earlier I should have stood in his shoes.

During these months I was grinding away at the four

subjects for the Second Professional, now looming in the near distance. Visiting the Infirmary wards was never neglected, this being, after all, the essential part of our training. One was meanwhile picking up experience, seeing fresh medical and surgical cases every day.

After my period at the eye ward ended, "clerking" in the surgical wards had to be done in the evenings. But as yet the medical wards had to remain over, for sheer want of time; one could not, like Sir Boyle Roche's bird, be in two places at once!

All these engagements, of course, involved a great amount of daily walking. This resulted in physical and nervous fatigue. We could not always afford to patronize the old three-horse bus, which was our sole means of transport, so had to trudge. The early morning hours, when one was fresh, and the world quiet, I found best for study; so when class examinations, or worse still the professional ones, were imminent, I would rise at four or five in the morning and plod away till breakfast-time.

Dissecting and Anatomical Demonstrations still went on — an appalling grind. In addition there was Practical Dispensing, which I took out at the Cowgate Dispensary in the Medical Mission there. This meant evening visits thither, to dispense the various prescriptions ordered during the afternoon consulting hour. Infusions, pills, plasters, powders, and mixtures all passed through our 'prentice hands; but providentially were supervised by our kindly and sagacious Head Chemist. Some funny things happened. One day a cryptic prescription came in for dispensing, which none of us could understand. It read thus: " *Recipe : Extract Stump.*" This mysterious note was passed round, but none could fathom its secret. The solution eventually proved to be an instruction, dictated by a doctor to a student acting as his clerk: "Extract stump of tooth." But the clerk, having already automatically written the word "Recipe," simply added: "Extract Stump"—no doubt believing this to be some unknown vegetable extract! I am reminded here of the patient who was startled by discovering the letters "R.I.P." inserted in parentheses on a prescription handed to him. As he braced himself for the worst, he stammered out: "No hope for me, then?"—and was hastily reassured that "R.I.P." stood for nothing more sinister than "Recipe according to Infirmary Pharmacopœia"!

We had one stock mixture for bronchitis; another for gastric catarrh, and two more, containing no poisons, and incapable of doing much harm if mistakenly prescribed for the wrong malady.

Here too, in the Cowgate Dispensary, I extracted my first tooth, and in doing so made two mistakes: I set the patient, a half-drunken Irishman, in front of the window in a cane chair which was far too light in construction. Then, without any preliminary manœuvres, but relying on force alone, I pulled the right upper molar as hard as I could. At first nothing happened; then, all of a sudden, I was flung violently back against the wall, and the Irishman, as violently, was thrown in a heap on the floor, the ruins of the chair on top of him. But my hand still grasped the forceps, which in turn still grasped the tooth!

In our final year at the University we used to attend the Friday Clinics held by Joseph Bell (the original of "Sherlock Holmes"), in the Royal Infirmary, in order to become acquainted with as many and as varied cases as possible. Bell's staff was so well organized that there was no loss of time; the patients, all prepared in the side-room, were run into the theatre at great speed, diagnosed and run out again. It was here that Conan Doyle, then an ordinary student like ourselves, observed, studied, and took notes, which he utilized thereafter in his stories. One young fellow, I remember, gave what was evidently a false name; but Jo Bell in writing the prescription calmly wrote down his real one and handed the paper to the patient. He blushed, looked sheepish, and departed. When he had gone, Jo said: "I daresay you all noticed what I did then; it was obvious that 'John Smith' was not his real name, but I saw the true name on his shirt-band." Thus he trained us, his amateur "Watsons," in the habit of observation.

One day a woman silently entered and, without speaking, handed to Bell a small vial, stoppered with a plug of soft paper, around which was wound some black thread. Jo immediately said: "Well, ma'am, so your man's a tailor? And how long has he been ill?" The woman looked surprised, and confirmed the information. When she had left, Jo remarked: "It was quite evident that this woman herself was not the patient; she was too well. She wore a wedding ring, but was not dressed as a widow. The vial was plugged with one of those stoppers of paper on which tailors wind their threads when in use."

On another occasion a man entered the clinic at a quick pace, and said nothing, but stood at attention. Without asking a single question, Bell diagnosed that he was a soldier recently home from the West Indies, with a skin trouble indigenous there. Evidence: his military entry, his silence till addressed; his sunburnt features; the white skin above the line of his cap, and the rash upon the skin characteristic of that particular disease.

Occasionally I attempted a little "Watsonian" sleuth work on my own. One night Sutherland and I ascended a stair in Candlemaker Row, where on a wretched bed lay a young man, evidently in a late stage of phthisis. The poor fellow was sweltering, with a heavy coat upon him beneath the ragged coverlet. We examined him in turn, and then, adopting the manner of Jo Bell, I asked him: "How long is it since you were a Volunteer?" He told me. On regaining the street

Sutherland said: "Clever of you to diagnose that he had been a Volunteer, after simply sounding his chest; how did you do it?" After tantalizing my companion awhile, I confessed; I had observed, peeping from below the coverlet, the button and black bugle crest of the Queen's Edinburgh Volunteer Brigade. Whereupon the disgruntled Sutherland merely exclaimed: "*Quack !*"

Conan Doyle, like myself, held an average position as a student, and was not specially brilliant. But curiously enough his name held a special fascination for me. When the Pass Lists were posted in the vestibule, I formed the odd habit of invariably looking for his name first of all, and when I descried that "Doyle" had passed I looked with greater hopefulness for "Gunn"!

One evening when walking home, during the celebrated Midlothian Campaign, I observed Mr Gladstone standing bolt upright in a rapidly moving carriage, bowing like an automaton to the excited crowds which thronged the thoroughfare.

In those days we students issued forth on our rounds from the Cowgate Dispensary, and, for the greater safety of our patients and of ourselves, hunted in pairs. One interesting maternity case Sutherland and I shared, at the top of a nine-storey turnpike stair, as steep as it was lofty, in a high "land" in the Lawnmarket. The patient was a young woman whose husband, if any, was stated to be a sailor, and therefore absent. There were then no professional nurses; the wise woman of the tenement presided over all, assisted by her gossips, who refreshed themselves with conversation flavoured with strong tea, which in turn was flavoured with whisky. One candle at the bedside and another on the mantelshelf furnished our sole light.

Away to the north through the clear frosty moonlight we could see the shadowy Firth of Forth, and the silver islets starring its broad bosom. Above, the stars

37

shone frostily, and the revolving gleam of Inchkeith Lighthouse, so familiar from my childhood days, lit up a picture of amazing beauty. So the night passed, and still we waited. Presently, between us, we had sufficient intuition to diagnose that all was not right, so sent for the assistance of Dr Berry Hart, then styled by us all "the berry hearty fellow."

He arrived in a cab, whose wheels were a delightful sound to our worried ears far aloft in the attic room. He was piloted up the long stair; examined the patient; redressed the wrong position; and finally delivered the girl of a still-born baby.

As Hugh and I desired to use the body as a subject for dissection, we wrapped it carefully in such coverings as could be procured, and after arranging the patient comfortably we all three descended to the waiting cab, placing the body beneath the seat. Away over the Lawnmarket cobbles the horse trotted, through the clear frosty winter's night. Suddenly our hearts all but ceased to beat, as a Punchinello squeak was heard beneath the seat, followed by an unmistakable cry. Out jumped Berry Hart immediately, with the terse remark: "I *turned* the child, you fellows may *re-turn* it!!" The jolting of the cab, and the cool frosty air, had combined to stimulate respiration in the infant, which had then decided to come to life! Shamefacedly Hugh and I slowly reascended the turnpike stair, somewhat dubious as to our reception. But we were received with grateful delight, and hailed as wonderful practitioners, the young mother's conviction being that we had taken the still-born infant away for the purpose of restoring it, and had miraculously succeeded! We both bowed with modest grace, accepted congratulations on our feat in becoming silence, and decorously withdrew. If the squeaker-hero of that occasion grew up, and survived the War, he must now be close on fifty years of age!

The customary Saturday-night street rows diversified our course at the Cowgate Dispensary. These served to train us in resourcefulness, calmness in the face of accident and danger, and presence of mind when menaced by excitable and drunken patients. We learned also when to be silent, and never to hazard any opinion in an assault case, which might prove to be of serious or criminal importance. Also we learned never to interfere in a row between husband and wife, as in every case, if we attacked the man, either verbally or by force, his suffering helpmeet would invariably take her husband's part, turning upon us with shrieks, scratchings, and menaces, and often attempting personal violence into the bargain.

In the Cowgate district, at the top of one of the familiar turnpike stairs, I one day found my progress barred by the form of an enormous fat pig, placidly engaged in eating tea-leaves. Straddling across its huge bulk, I questioned the owner, an agreeable Irishman, as to its history. "How in the world did you manage to get this huge beast up such a stair?" "Sure, Doctor," replied Pat, "he never was down: he was born here!"

Early in 1882, at the age of twenty-one, I passed the Final Examinations in Medicine. The fateful verdict was conveyed to me by the postman as I knelt weeding the avenue of Stichill Manse, like a modern Cincinnatus. Palpitating with excitement and pallid from the shock of the good news, I entered the village church and there, with the earnestness of early piety, thanked God for this culmination of years of struggle and hopeful endeavour.

That same day I sent in my name as an applicant for any likely assistantship, and awaited results.

Then followed a brief halcyon period of entire relaxation—the first in my life, and, as seems likely, the last! I was sure of my degree, and had nothing to think about but my forthcoming entry into practice, save the ceremony of Graduation looming ahead. I spent those golden summer weeks at Stichill, in my brother's home; it was a time of complete and unalloyed companionship —the last he and I were destined to enjoy alone together. Our lives had given little opportunity for leisure up to this point, so he and I made the most of these too-short weeks of tranquil summer serenity.

After some time a reply came anent an assistantship; the agent announced a vacancy at Newburgh-on-Tay. Little did he regard himself, in so doing, as the arbiter of Fate!

To me a river had ever seemed a desirable neighbour, as running water, wherefore I know not, held for me a poetic fascination. Therefore, when a study of the map revealed the situation of the town to be on the estuary of the Tay, my hesitation gave place to resolve. Then followed a tremulous journey, the prelude to a personal interview with the local doctor. What a day! Rain fell steadily all the way through Fife, and during transit across the Granton Ferry. Sunlight there was none; mist enshrouded the horizon and the distant hills. The train swept suddenly round the base of a lofty craig, and beneath my vision lay a dreary swamp of rainswept sand and mud, on which dun waves were beating.

Descending to the town, and entering a butcher's shop, I inquired where the doctor lived. "Is it himsel' ye mean? Yon's his poplars." Toward a distant row of eight sentinel poplars I directed my steps, to a short avenue in front of a neat villa. A young man was earnestly shooting sparrows on the front. From him came a friendly nod. "The doctor is out, but will return soon. I am his present assistant." Then from the doorway came the doctor's housekeeper, who, unknown to herself, was destined to foster-mother me for the next three years. "Buxom and bonere," to borrow

Chaucer's phrase, describes her best, with her sonsy face, brown kindly eyes, and plump figure.

"Come your ways in," was her greeting, the first of many such in days to come.

It was not long ere the doctor arrived, a bearded man, square of build, of ruddy countenance, and with piercing blue eyes, dressily clad in a smart black velvet jacket and vest. We said little, but took one another for granted; I left duly engaged as his assistant-elect, to begin my duties immediately after the coming Graduation.

GRADUATION DAY was 1st August 1882. The ceremony
took place in the United Presbyterian Synod Hall, and
the "capping" was performed by the Lord Chancellor
Inglis, President of the Court of Session. One magic
touch on the head from the revered and traditional
velvet breeches, formerly worn by George Buchanan,
and the deed was done!

My mother and my eldest brother were present at
this launching of the youngest member of the family,
who thus passed out of their self-denying care and
responsibility, into a world which he now entered on
his own.

Certain regrets were inevitable in parting with the
good friends of the last five years. Among them was
my *fidus Achates*, good Hugh Sutherland, with his
stirring accounts on Monday mornings in the class-
room of his week-end gallantries among the fair! He
it was who impressed me greatly by frequent rhapsodies
on "the ineffable shrug of Clytie's ivory shoulders,"
while I was still too unsophisticated to recognize his
plagiarism from *Trilby*!

To Hawarden, with its Gladstonian tradition, Hugh
went after Graduation; within a year he died of
tuberculosis.

Early tragedy cut short the life of William Thyne
also, in an even more dramatic way. Soon after he
left College he was recommended to take a voyage for
his health's sake before entering on practice. He sailed
for New Zealand as surgeon on board S.S. *Lochfyne*.
On her return journey from Christchurch the vessel
disappeared, and was never heard of again. Both

Thyne's parents were broken-hearted, and died soon after. So passed in the springtime of life a kindly comrade and rare soul.

After Graduation, then, we good companions parted, most of us never to meet again. There was more than a touch of sadness in those farewells. I never saw one of them again. Even yet I note regretfully, from time to time in the daily Press, the dropping out of one more of the Ancient Band.

The instant that the lengthy ceremonies ended, I rushed off to the Waverley Station and took train for Newburgh-on-Tay. No time even to change my dress clothes, *de rigueur* at Graduation, for more ordinary garb!

Something of heartsickness there was, after bidding my mother farewell, in this adventurous rush towards the unknown! But it was a sunny afternoon, and the fresh sea-breezes of the Forth, as we crossed the Burnt-island Ferry, refreshed and stimulated one's exhausted emotions. The broad estuary of the Tay scintillated in the westering sun; Ben Ledi and Ben Voirlich were silhouetted in a golden haze. The reeds fringing Mugdrum Island seemed instinct with life, gently swaying in the breeze.

One looked down upon the poplar-sentinelled Denmiln Castle, and on what appeared to be the rose-red walls of some ancient abbey. I had ever longed to live by a river; but for me to have this wish gratified, with an abbey thrown in, seemed too good to be true.

No one met me on arrival, so leaving my modest luggage to its own devices I made for the familiar row of poplars, and this time found the doctor at home. "You!" he exclaimed. "Already? Surely you want a few days' holiday before beginning work? Haven't you this moment graduated?"

Beneath my light overcoat he had espied the "swallow-tail" and white tie of Graduation, still unchanged! But to me, aged twenty-one, "life was real, life was earnest," with a vengeance! *O tempora! O mores!*

After tea, the doctor took me for a walk "round the fence," the earthen-turfed embankment which restrains the waters of the Firth within their proper bed. The setting sun, behind the lofty Grampian bens, sped brilliant shafts of gold and crimson down the valley of the Tay; it seemed a light that never was on sea or land. The glamour of mystery brooded over the Carse of Gowrie, laved by the tides of the lordly river.

On we strolled beside the tall whispering reeds. "And over there," said the doctor, "is the Abbey of Lindores."

Curfew was ringing from the town steeple, its chimes borne softly along the river's highway; and the music of the bells, with the cadence of the ancient abbey's name, lingered long in my mind.

The hill where we stood, the doctor told me, was called Mount Pleasant, and the fresh green boughs we saw everywhere were those of pear-trees.

I fell asleep that night with pleasant thoughts of beginning my life's work in a place so beautiful, meditating that the lines had indeed fallen unto me in pleasant places.

Little did I suspect that this was the last night's sound sleep that I was destined to enjoy for a long time!

Next morning I discovered that my duties as assistant were to include all the night work of the practice; of which more anon.

The doctor kept no fewer than four horses: two for his own carriage, one for his gig, and one (a grey mare with white eyelashes and bent fore-legs) for his assistant. When, not without trepidation, I mounted this animal for the first time the whole household assembled to see the fun. The doctor himself, his brother, Cely the housekeeper, with the "tweeny-maid" peeping over her shoulder: all came out to give me a send-off.

After cantering for a mile or two I drew rein to inquire the way, and was informed by an aged carle, very deaf, that I should proceed "by the north side of all the kirks" and would then find my destination.

With cramped limbs, a sinking of the heart (for the grey mare was distressingly fresh), and complete uncertainty as to the number and whereabouts of "all the kirks," I fetched a compass, as St Paul has it, carefully skirting four kirks in succession. Finally, weary, worn, and sad, but unbeaten, I arrived at the desired haven, only to receive the disconcerting greeting: "Who are you, laddie? And where is the Doctor?

Gloomily dismounting, I announced myself as "the new assistant," whereupon admission to the sickroom was doubtfully granted; and my professional life, properly speaking, began.

As the weeks passed, I gained confidence in the equestrian art, and could afford to use both spur and switch occasionally, so as to indicate to the mare that I was no longer novice, but master. One day, however, the unexpected happened.

I had made a journey along the beautiful hillside route by the Tay, and returning had reached a winding, narrow roadway, and was trotting merrily homeward, when all of a sudden there was I prone on my back in the dust, with the mare kicking her heels in the offing! Collecting hat and switch, I was dismally trudging homewards, when lo! the doctor approached, riding the runaway beast.

He had been placidly dining, but on hearing the sound of a distant gallop had sent Cely flying out to reconnoitre.

"Eh, Lord save us, Doctor," cried she, "it's the grey mare, and nobody on her back!" So the doctor had rushed forth, caught the runaway making for her stall,

45

and instantly mounting her, rode forth to collect the fragments of his assistant. With what nonchalance I could muster I greeted him gaily, quite as if my mode of dismounting had been adopted by personal preference. It appeared that, at a sudden bend of the road, the mare had shied at the unexpected sight of four harvesters carrying brightly polished milk-cans, on which the sun was shining with dazzling effect.

Three local dispensations of Providence, at this epoch, afforded signal delight to a city-bred boy like myself, who had seldom seen, and never lived in, the country. These were the Pears; the Salmon; and the Sparlings.

The pear orchards of Newburgh are the successors of those introduced and planted in mediæval times by the monks of Lindores Abbey, and almost every house in the town possesses such an orchard. Apples do not grow well there, but flourish in the adjacent Carse of Gowrie; hence the Newburgh boys will not steal pears, which are too common, but prefer the rarer apple.

Newburgh is built upon a slope, with Mount Pleasant rising behind, and the estuary of the Tay beneath. One result is that in springtime the whole town, as viewed from the hill, or from a boat on the river, is embowered in a wealth of pear-blossom, in variegated pink and white. The scene appears more like a glimpse of fairyland than of a plain Scottish town. Some of the names of these pears (for example, *bon-chrétiens*) recall their monkish origin. It was then not uncommon for a tree to bear as many as ninety stones of pears, at twenty-two pounds to the stone. The fallen pears were the perquisites of the horses and pigs; the others were munched by ourselves all day and every day— a rare treat.

And as if this were not enough for one small town to enjoy, there were the salmon-fishing banks. In August these were at their very best, and it was good sport to get into a coble, row out to a bank, and watch the men hauling in the nets laden with glittering, writhing fish; then to select one to be put into the pot, cooked, and eaten forthwith.

At the close of the season we had the salmon pickled with sugar and salt: a pleasant, toothsome delicacy for the winter breakfast-table, reminiscent of the bygone sunny autumn days.

Lastly, to complete this gastronomic paradise, there were the sparlings, which followed the salmon, and were in excellent condition just when the salmon-fishing closed. These were elongated silver fish, semi-transparent, and a great delicacy. They were packed into flat boxes as soon as caught, and, like the salmon, hurried off by special trains to the London market.

Behold us then, in the months of August and September, undergoing what I came to call the salmon-cure, the pear-cure, and the sparling-cure. Gratefully often I used to muse on the fact that had I become a colliery doctor (as at one time seemed possible) these delightful gifts of Nature would have remained unknown to me.

At Newburgh I soon became accustomed to the routine of daily duty. At nine each morning the Dispensary opened. Thither I proceeded, to dispense medicines and drugs to all and sundry. Thereafter I saddled the grey mare, and as a rule rode "west." This meant towards Abernethy and the adjoining region, which lies in the county of Perth.

In the afternoon we "did" the town, each independently visiting his own part of the practice without overlapping. Before starting, I devoted another hour to the Dispensary; the last attendance there was from six to seven o'clock. On all these occasions advice was given, as well as drugs made up.

It was a strenuous life, and work seemed never-ending. My salary as assistant was £80 per annum. All the night duty was discharged by me, at all seasons and in all weathers.

When on horseback one could not carry lights, but had to trust to the horse's instinct in avoiding dangerous parts of the road. There was no tar macadam, nor electric torches, then, and the risks were many. Occasionally mists descended, and so obscured the atmosphere that one became bewildered and lost. Sometimes, on finding the wall of a cottage, I had to dismount, tap at the window, and ask the suddenly aroused inmates where I was.

All maternity instruments were carried in one's many pockets; and on stormy or snowy nights a riding-cape covered all. It was never possible to make up sleep, for on returning in the morning, after bath and breakfast, one had to resume the daily round, the common task. I often wore my riding-boots and spurs throughout the day, and folks remarked that the Assistant slept in them.

Looking back, I am inclined to think that these Fife maternity cases were unduly protracted and severe, and that this was possibly due to local conditions of existence, as many of the mothers spent their days sitting at the handlooms weaving linen, and took little other exercise. When I went first to Newburgh one might hear at the mouth of every wynd the rattle of the shuttle; now there is not one surviving, their place having been taken by steam-power in mills.

Three dogs accompanied me on my daily rounds on horseback: Nell, a greyhound, Dizzy, a Scotch terrier, and Jock, a wire-haired mongrel. Dizzy and Jock invariably behaved well, and passed their time in the open while I was engaged with a patient; but, despite all my efforts at discipline, the greyhound never failed to obtain entrance, not merely to the house, but to the sickroom, where, with one swift silent leap, she would ensconce herself on the bed. Her interest in my professional methods never diminished!

So our daily cavalcade proceeded: greyhound Nell ever in the front line, myself next on the grey mare, the Scotch terrier scampering alongside, and wire-haired Jock all over the place, chasing every rabbit and cat we encountered. The nightly clatter of our hoofs on the causeway of the long High Street wakened the douce Newburgh burgesses, who doubtless turned in their warm beds with the drowsy comment: "There's the Assistant away by." Often I waked the midnight echo against the lofty cliff of Clatchart, as I rode eastwards in the silent night.

I was ever a light sleeper, and would usually wake on hearing, at first distantly, then nearer and nearer, the ominous plod-plodding of some ploughman's horse steadily approaching the doctor's house. The messenger's purposeful tread down the short avenue followed; then the noisy jangling of the bell. Up would go the blind to ascertain the kind of weather, and whether or not there was a moon; then a hurried dressing, unlocking the stable door, rousing the sleepy horse; on with saddle and bridle, and so away on my lonely ride.

One very long journey I recall with great vividness, owing to a curious circumstance which fixed it for ever in my mind. My destination was a place called Lindifferon—a name which, to the best of my belief, I had never before heard. The country through which I passed was strange to me; there was one ancient tower, I remember, with roof-beams still displaying the painted escutcheons, faded and time-worn, of a long-vanished lineage. Suddenly I came in sight of an old mill with black, tattered sails, and a red-roofed farm-house near it; and instantly I knew, "This is Lindifferon." Every feature of the place, though never before seen, was intimately familiar to me—the

49

ancient derelict mill, the red tiles of the farm-dwellings, the clear stream flowing past. All seemed to pass through my mind like a remembered dream. Yet I had never set foot in the place before.

Years afterwards, my mother, to whom I related this odd experience, told me that she and my father had, before my birth, spent a short holiday at that very place: Lindifferon. The mill, the stream, and every detail of the picturesque surroundings had been indelibly impressed on her mind, for an experience she had at that time nearly ended in disaster. While they were enjoying a pleasure-trip aboard a pinnace, the water became so rough, and my mother so much alarmed, that she flung her arms round one of the boatmen for protection, he being nearer for this purpose than her unperturbed husband. "Hoots, mem!" the stalwart mariner callously exclaimed, "dae ye no' think we hae a' lives to lose as weel as you?"

We had at this time as a patient an ancient of ninety-seven years, who lived in a neat flower-covered cottage several miles along the Tayside road. He always insisted on a visit every second day; and if under pressure of work this was omitted, he never failed to send an urgent summons in the evening.

The special routine of these visits never varied. Fastening the mare to a convenient ring near the cottage door, I would enter, and bellow into his ear (he was stone-deaf): "How are you to-day?" To which his invariable answer, shouted at the pitch of his voice, was: "Ten thoosand times waur!" "Right; go on as you are doing!" I would yell, and ride off again. For eighteen months this routine continued unbroken, till eventually the aged pessimist passed on.

Another patient was an old farmer, very seriously ill. The doctor one day conveyed to him in his gig a case of aerated waters, for which the old man had expressed a great longing. As the doctor was carrying the heavy case from the gig down a longish farm-road toward the house, the patient's daughter met him with a very long face: "Eh, Doctor," she said, in melancholy tones, "ye're too late now; too late." Naturally the doctor inferred that the old man had died, and after expressing decorous regret turned away with his bottles, when the woman suddenly cried out: "We sent to Cupar for fizzy drinks on Saturday night, and they cured him, so we dinna' need yours!" The impatient patient rapidly recovered.

One afternoon, while we were enjoying the unaccustomed relaxation of a game of bowls on the doctor's lawn, a small boy was brought in, with a hard sweet lodged in his larynx. It was suggested that I ascend the garden seat with the boy inverted in my arms, and jump with him to the ground. After many attempts we were all relieved by the reappearance of the hard almond sweet, which dropped out, rattling against his teeth. But before we could prevent him, the reckless rascal had pursued it as it rolled away on the grass, and instantly popped it again into his mouth, where no doubt it took the correct course, as we did not see the young economist again.

On a similar occasion, I once observed Jo Bell ("Sherlock Holmes"), in an operating theatre, when the house surgeon jumped off the table, holding an inverted boy in his arms. The coin, which was a sixpenny-bit, dropped out of the larynx and rolled along the floor; Bell swiftly picked it up and pocketed it, remarking quietly: "This is the only fee I'll get."

When riding on my rounds one day I met a small procession, consisting of an elderly woman carrying an infant, accompanied by one or two neighbours. "Beg pardon, Doctor," the first woman called out, "but ye maun tak' the Bairn's Piece!" She thereupon handed to me a ration of biscuit and cheese. I had wit enough to accept it, and to present to the young catechumen on

51

his way to baptism a reddendo of silver to bring good luck.

Funerals in the neighbourhood were then a great source of diversion to many elderly men, and formed almost their sole distraction from monotony. The town bell always tolled as the *cortège* was passing, and the house of mourning was indicated by a sheet or large towel covering the lower half of the windows. The burgh elders would await the hearse in front of the Town Hall, join ranks, and proceed eastward to the cemetery beyond the town.

One old man, by trade a joiner and undertaker, frequently annoyed me by inquiring in a professional manner how such-and-such a patient was getting on. Was he or she any better? This show of compassionate interest puzzled me somewhat. The doctor, however, explained that our friend the undertaker had a keen eye for a job, and suggested that to his next anxious inquiry I should retort: "What about Mrs So-and-So's coffin?" Which I did; the counter-stroke was received with loud profanity. It appeared that, some years earlier, our zealous friend had become aware that a certain aged lady was likely to die at any moment. So, with commendable business instinct, he rapidly constructed her coffin in readiness for the sad event. She however recovered; so the unwanted article reposed for many years upon the rafters above the joiner's shop: a perfect specimen of that rare object, a second-hand coffin.

Among my various duties in the Dispensary were three which caused me much trouble: pills, plasters, and ointments. These articles had to be manufactured (literally) by hand. For the pills, there was what is called the excipient to be produced, from breadcrumb and treacle; to this was added the medicament, in powder or extract; the whole mass was then rolled out into a long cylindrical strip, which when chopped small, and rolled into the shape of pills, was dried with powdered sugar or French chalk. The results of my labours generally resembled small bullets, rather than regulation pellets. But these products were cheerfully swallowed, the recipients little knowing that the finished article had been conscientiously rolled between the palms of the Assistant's hands!

For plasters, a measured area of sheepskin was first cut out. Then a thick stick of plaster (like a policeman's baton) was softened at the fire, and portions of this were spread with a spatula on the sheepskin—a messy job.

The ointments were made in the kitchen, where Cely the housekeeper placed a large pot of melted lard on the fire. The oily liquid was then poured into a gallipot, and a weighed quantity of zinc oxide or other powder poured into it. This was vigorously stirred by each of us in turn, the gradually cooling mass becoming thicker and more difficult to move about, so that the united efforts of Cely, the tweeny-maid, and the Assistant were required ere the ointment became completely homogeneous.

Tinctures and infusions, too, had to be filtered; and our leeches exercised along the counter. Regarding these animals, the following tale was current at the time. A doctor had ordered six leeches to be applied to a man's stomach after bathing the skin in sweet milk. Accordingly, to an inquiry as to her method of procedure, the patient's wife answered: "Dinna be angry, Doctor; we first of all poured the milk down to his stomach, but he couldna swallow a' the leeches raw, so we just fried the other three"!

About this period I was presented with the gift of two owls. This necessitated my constructing an aviary in the orchard, in which to house them. The open front was protected by trellis-work and the structure was six feet in height. The owls, perched in their retreat, received many visits from passing schoolchildren, who were wont to bring them mice at the rate of one penny for a big mouse; a halfpenny for a wee one; mixed sizes at two for three-halfpence.

At this season of the year the country where my lot was cast was lovely both by day and night. By day, there were the pleasant wooded shores, vivid with the chromatic colours of late autumn, which girdled the fertile Carse. In the background towered the Grampian range; the steeples of many country churches dotted the landscape; the Tay, with its island in the midst, was calm as glass; here and there a sloop or fishing-boat would float on the unruffled surface.

By night, the moon and a thousand stars were reflected in the silent river—a nocturne in blue and silver. Lower down, at Newport, loomed the ruined Tay Bridge, with its ghastly, sinister gap silhouetted in black against the eastern sky. Here and there, a stray boat-light flecked the bosom of the water, as the night fishers plied their silent, solitary task.

I often visited the haunted Black Loch, which well deserved its name. I must confess that it was never given to me to meet the sad-visaged ghost in sober grey, which local tradition described as flitting like a giant moth up the avenue of the mansion-house. Nor did I ever hear the splash as she vanished into the depths of the haunted loch. One old grandam often told me that her husband, accompanied by his faithful collie, did actually see and hear this apparition, while the dog crouched terror-stricken at his master's feet. Also a maid employed at the mansion-house told me that a ghostly face had more than once peered at her through a window, and vanished when observed.

When visiting professionally at Lindores House I was wont to listen attentively for the rumbling of the phantom hearse, which betokened the approaching demise of the Laird. I was never rewarded by any spectacular sight; perhaps because the Laird was then non-resident, and the house temporarily let.

During the severe winter which now opened, the doctor, for a wager, drove his sleigh and pair of horses across the full length of Loch Lindores without accident.

After heavy snow had lain for a day or two and had become frozen, we paid our professional visits in the sleigh, and with the roan horse in the shafts, and the bells going merrily, would speed along the roads at a great pace. It was a pleasant, restful change from riding; and the music of the bells in the frosty air had a most exhilarating effect upon the spirits.

At the annual Curling Dinner, which the doctor regularly attended, the raising of needful funds customarily took place in the form of fines imposed upon the members. During my first season as his assistant, the doctor's contribution was facetiously extorted as "the fine for keeping a Gunn without a licence"!

Lindores Loch, however, soon proved the arena of my personal struggles in a romantic cause. Among the throng of skaters whom I often observed when passing the loch on my daily rounds was one who intrigued me much. This lady, hazel-eyed, with Grecian features and a complexion of magnolia-blossom, would glide gracefully along the glassy surface in the frosty winter sunlight; usually alone, but sometimes with an accompanying male, whom I urgently desired to put to death. Instead of gratifying this natural wish, I forthwith resolved to learn to skate, and that without delay. Night after night, therefore, I secretly made my way to the shores of the loch, and there for hours, in solitude and darkness, and with grave risk to life and limb, I practised the graceful movements which seemed so easy in others, but were, alas, so foreign to me! Usually I chose a moonless night for these gyrations, as there was less risk of being discovered, though perhaps greater fear of being drowned! It may as well be confessed sooner as later, that, despite prolonged nocturnal struggles, graceful proficiency as a skater was for ever beyond me. But I succeeded in my purpose of displacing my rival, if not on the ice, at any rate as a life-partner; for the lady in whose honour I dared the dangers of Lindores Loch on so many dark and dismal nights, eventually became my wife.

In dancing, also, I now resolved to acquire skill, both in order to oust other partners from the side of my adored, and to avail myself of the opportunities for meeting her which the winter social gatherings afforded.

One of these occasions is stamped for ever on my memory, for, greatly daring, though aware of my imperfections as a partner, I essayed to dance with Her—a vision of delight, gowned in palest eau-de-nil. It was a country-dance, and my deficiencies, therefore, were not at first apparent; I hopped back and forth gaily enough, in a kind of ecstatic trance. Later, however, I rashly begged for a waltz. She acquiesced; and waltz we did. But alas! I was rigid as a wooden image. In vain I murmured inwardly the mystic incantation of the dancing-school (where I had been sedulously taking lessons for many weeks): "One, two, three; four, five, six!" In vain I performed every step, every figure, with rigorous exactitude, correct and foot-perfect as on the class-room floor! I was only too well aware that my fair partner was not happy; and as the moments passed I too sank into an abyss of misery. On we struggled, rotating in grim silence, every step meticulously performed by me, and bravely responded to by Her. Conversation languished. Our relief when the music ceased was mutual and unconcealed. For the rest of the evening I had to endure the pain of watching Her enjoyably waltzing with more graceful and accomplished partners.

But this sad experience confirmed my resolve: I *would* learn to dance, cost what it might, rather than continue to stand tamely by and view Her in the clasp of others. So from that day forward, in addition to nightly rehearsals conducted in the solitude of my room, I practised the waltz as opportunity offered, in the open air when on my rounds. I would select a secluded by-road, screened from observation by trees, and having made certain that not a soul was in sight, would dismount, fasten the reins to a fence, and doggedly begin my joyless chant: "One, two, three; four, five, six!" Round and round I spun like a top, completely oblivious of the beauties of nature about me, my one object in life to achieve a graceful rhythmic "glide," and to avoid the automatic jerkings of the drill-sergeant. Week after week this exercise continued, and still no "glide" resulted; those accursed steps haunted me day and night. Yet, though with considerably more courage than success, I persevered.

In addition to my owls, I now acquired a new pet, in the shape of a tiny brown-eyed monkey, whom I christened Jerry. He enjoyed a happy existence beneath the poplars in the avenue, in a large hut with a plate-glass window, with a shelf behind, where he sat making observations on the passers-by. Round his waist hung a very light chain, long enough to allow him to ascend the walnut-tree beside his hut, whence he would descend with handfuls of green walnuts.

Unfortunately, as the colder weather came on, he contracted croup, and despite doses of ipecacuanha-wine rapidly became worse. I made a warm coat for him, which he contemptuously tore off; and despite unwearying efforts to save him, he died one Christmas, to my deep regret. He passed, I am sure, straight to the monkeys' Valhalla of unlimited nuts and convenient branches.

About this time one of my owls followed the monkey's example, and died. I had the unique inspiration of having him stuffed in a very handsome manner, and of presenting him to my lady-love. Was ever such a love-gage proffered before? Or since?

I borrowed a brief-bag from a lawyer friend, in which to convey my offering to the lady's house. Some time afterwards he and I were bidden to an evening party there, and on entering the drawing-room together we beheld the stuffed owl, in all its glory, perched high in a corner opposite the door. Instantly the lawyer convulsed the company by remarking: "*Now* at last I know why my bag was borrowed; it was to hold that owl!" To that bird I pinned my hopes of successful courtship; so long as he remained secure on his perch, I felt that I need not despair. One of my worst moments occurred when once I observed that the perch was vacant; I immediately became suicidal, only to find that the owl had been temporarily removed during spring-cleaning operations!

At every concert where my lady-love was expected to sing—and such were frequent, as she had a beautiful and expressive contralto voice—I contrived to be present. If the entertainment were at a distance I usually arranged to have a visit in the neighbour-hood, or a convenient baby to be vaccinated hard by. On one occasion I attended a lengthy lecture on Mohammed the Prophet solely for the purpose of escorting my fair companion home. At length, taking courage from Montrose's lines—

> He either fears his fate too much,
> Or his deserts are small,
> Who dares not put it to the touch
> To gain or lose it all—

I applied them to my own case, and with success. We became engaged, and I was thus in a fair way to carry off as my bride the lady whom I had determined to win from the first moment of seeing her, and had long ago pointed out to my mother as her daughter-in-law-to-be, before we had ever held speech with one another.

I now began to make widespread inquiries for a vacant practice elsewhere. Many places were suggested and considered, among them Peebles, where there were at that time only two doctors in the field.

At this time I attended a number of Norwegian sailors on board ship in the harbour. This was a novel experience, as we had no interpreter, and all diagnosis had to be carried through by observation alone. There was about this time a very bad fever outbreak at Abernethy, whither I rode twice or thrice daily. It was a quaint interesting village, with its unique Round Tower close to the Parish Church, its Licker Stanes on which dead bodies were formerly laid, and its vitrified Picts' Tower. This place had in former days a great theological reputation; at the time of the first secession from the Church of Scotland the inhabitants thought nothing of travelling twenty miles every Sunday to take part in public worship. One of their oddest pious practices was that of praying and singing aloud, in harvest-time, behind the stooks of corn. The whole atmosphere, it is said, resounded with the sonorous boomings of these open-air worshippers. Whether this habit was due to genuine pious enthusiasm on the seceders' part, or was adopted as a protest of the "unco guid" against their more easy-going brethren of the "Auld Kirk," is not easy to determine.

I had occasion while in Newburgh to meet in consultation the eminent Professor Grainger Stewart, of Edinburgh. He it was who informed his University class one morning that he had been appointed Physician to H.M. Queen Victoria, whereupon his students rose as one man and sang with immense fervour: *God save the Queen*!

It was recorded of him also that an old Highland minister, who had unsuccessfully begged a subscription from him for some charity, passed on to a fellow-professor and told his tale. "And what did you say to the Professor of Medicine when he refused you?" asked this colleague.

"I told him he was just a hell-deserving sinner like mysel'."

"You told him that? Good! Here are ten pounds for you!"

My lawyer friend (he of the borrowed brief-bag) told me one day that he had just been attending a Fife funeral, at which the officiating minister, after the grave-side rites, immediately approached him, as the deceased's man of business, with the portentous inquiry: "*Who is to get the silver teapot?*" Such a spiritual adviser might well have adorned the pages of Galt.

My last visit in the Newburgh practice was one which I remember clearly to this day. I paid it on horseback, passing near the Cross Macduff, that mysterious monolith on the watershed of the wide pass leading from Fife to Strathearn. That night the glen where the Cross stands was awesome and memorable; against the brilliant streamers of an aurora borealis the Cross was silhouetted, stark and commanding. It was down this solitary pass that Macduff fled, pursued by Macbeth; here, too, many another man-slayer has been hunted and harried till he has at length found sanctuary at the Cross. In my mind, as I paused there, the prophetic words of Sir Walter found an echo:

> None shall pass
> Now, or in after days, beside that Stone
> But he shall have strange visions: thoughts and words
> That shake or rouse or thrill the human heart
> Shall rush upon his memory.

Bound as I now was upon a new unknown adventure, with my face set towards the far-away uplands of Tweed, I had plenty of "strange visions" to bear me company. And many a time in after years the recollection of that last vigil by the ancient Fifeshire Cross, with the thoughts that then thronged my youthful mind, has "rushed upon my memory" in unforgotten enchantment.

On the following day I left Newburgh, having been assistant there for three-and-a-half years.

What had I gained meanwhile? First, I had mastered the practical basis of my profession, the art and craft of medicine, which begins and develops only after a man leaves University and Hospital.

Secondly, I had endured an extremely severe training and initiation: the very best I could have had. It not only made one exact, punctual, and methodical; but taught one to "thole" hardship, exposure, disappointment, and sorrow without complaint. It also taught me the value of initiative, and the lifelong habit of self-reliance when in difficulty.

During these years I learned, besides many practical matters such as expert horsemanship, to be silent when necessary, to keep my own counsel, and to confide in no one; to believe nothing that I heard, and only half of what I saw! I learned also to be patient under the vagaries and idiosyncrasies of all manner of patients; I endeavoured to be helpful and sympathetic; above all, I strove to develop and to sustain a sense of humour —not the least vital asset in professional life!

In October 1885, then, I bade farewell to the old Abbey, with its historic associations and romantic memories; to Lindores Loch, the scene of my youthful escapades of triumph and disaster; and went forth from the ancient Kingdom of Fife to seek fresh experiences among the unknown uplands of the Scottish Borders.

CHAPTER IV   THE BRASS PLATE GOES UP—THE
FIRST PATIENT—MARRIAGE AND
"MAKING A PRACTICE"

AT Peebles I now embarked upon a new stage of my
adventures, little thinking how many years of my life
were to be passed among the friendly hills and green
pastures of Tweeddale.

I left two large boxes of books at the station, and
proceeded in leisurely fashion along the High Street,
a stranger in a strange land. On the advice of the
minister, the Rev. John Bell Lorraine, I engaged
rooms opposite the manse (which then stood at the
head of the Old Town); and by nightfall my belongings were installed, my mother informed by letter of
my arrangements, and a large brass plate ordered for
the gate.

Having thus settled in I began the arduous task of
"making a practice." For a time it seemed as though
this would consist chiefly in waiting for that momentous
event, the arrival of the First Patient! I hesitated at
first to leave the house even for half-an-hour, in case
The Patient might arrive in my absence! But prudence
counselled the necessity of being seen abroad, so that
prospective patients might judge for themselves of
the new medical acquisition gained by the town.
Accordingly, twice daily, I sallied forth in full panoply
of tile hat, top-coat and gloves; walked rapidly
through the town in all directions; then hastened
homewards, eager to know whether The Patient had
arrived.

The days passed, and the weeks likewise; still no
Patient! I extended my daily rounds, now mounted
in the afternoons upon a tricycle lent to me by one
of my brothers, and visited various outlying villages,

62

partly with a view to exploring their churches (some of them ancient and full of interest), and partly in the hope that observers might believe the new doctor to be already gratifyingly busy.

In the evenings, as a diversion, I wrote my reminiscences of school life, and christened these "Memories of a Modern Monk." They appeared in the *Scottish News* in serial form, and were afterwards published as a book. I also busied myself with a lecture on Chatterton. One night, persuaded by the minister and his wife, I attended an amateur theatrical performance in the Chambers Hall. The main piece was *Guy Mannering*, very fairly acted; but what struck home to me more forcibly was a farce called *The Irish Doctor*, where a new practitioner, engaged like myself in building up a practice, languished long without a single patient, and when they at last arrived, dismayed them by demanding his fees in advance ere he would consent to diagnose.

With my equestrian experiences in Fife fresh in my mind, I now set about making inquiries for a horse, not for any immediate purpose, but in the hope of extensive country journeys to come.

Each week was brightened by cheerful and encouraging letters from my mother at Stichill and from my fiancée at Newburgh. These letters were my tonic and stimulant at this time, and buoyed me up to continue my uphill task.

At length, after six weary weeks—enter *The Patient*! My satisfaction at this event, so eagerly awaited, was in no way marred by the fact that the Patient, when at long last she came, proved to be a person by no means universally respected, and extremely unlikely to pay a fee. Enough for me that I had secured one *bona-fide* patient, of whatever condition; proudly I marched beside her all along the High Street, displaying my captive in the full light of day.

Whilst we were thus engaged, who should pass but one of the other local doctors, who closely observed our walk and conversation. That evening at the manse I was greeted by the minister with the jovial cry: "So *The Patient* has come at last!" It appeared that my professional brother had hastened to impart the glad tidings without loss of time; and had added that the new doctor was more than welcome to that particular patient and all her "set"! The "set" certainly followed suit as predicted; within a week I was inundated by the patient's "sisters and her cousins and her aunts." But no matter; it was a beginning, and led to better things.

Towards the close of my first few months in Peebles I attended a function—my first form of dissipation since my arrival—known as the Volunteer Ball. I was persuaded to attend by the minister, who was himself a beautiful dancer, and enjoyed such an evening like the youngest of his flock. His hearty laugh and boyish spirits were infectious, and prevented anything like dullness in his neighbourhood. Girls of all ranks were in evidence at this function, partnered by private soldiers and officers as well. From the walls of the ball-room hung the flags of all nations; the Volunteer officers appeared in full war-paint, gorgeously trimmed with silver lace; the rank and file were a blaze of scarlet; the civilian guests made a striking contrast in their regulation black and white.

Presently, the "Ring Master," a burly sergeant, bellowed in stentorian tones as though addressing recruits on the parade-ground: "Choose pairtners for the Grand March!" Instantly all was chaos; the hall became a seething mass of kaleidoscopic colour, with the brilliant banners floating gaily overhead. Mars sought the arms of Venus at express speed—in other words, every man the damsel of his choice, on whom he had been keeping a jealous eye during the preceding moments. Round we marched in pairs, enlivened by the orchestra's gayest strains; up the centre, where we divided, "male and female each after his kind," and thus proceeded in single file (in order, doubtless, to display the ladies' dresses), till reunited at length, when by a complicated manœuvre we "formed fours," and the Grand March was brought to a successful conclusion.

In a letter to my mother describing the ceremonies I appended the results of my observations during the Grand March: "About forty tarlatan dresses of all shades, four lace dresses, two of oatmeal-cloth, all semi-decolletées. Other dresses of silk, net, or satin, with a good deal of jewelry and flowers."

Early in the new year, 1886, occurred a snowstorm of historic magnitude, long to be remembered throughout the Borders. On the 1st of March snow fell all day, clearing slightly about five o'clock, only to redouble its force during the long hours of the night. By daybreak next morning nothing could be seen but snow; the wind rose, and great drifts formed. It was the day of the March Fair, and attempts were made to erect stalls as usual on the streets; but no trade was done, for it was impossible to maintain the stalls in position. The Fair therefore came to a premature end. The railways very soon became blocked, and the train due at Peebles at noon failed to penetrate the deep drifts in its path.

The gale was now raging with great fury, and all attempts to clear the line by means of the snow-plough were ineffectual. The snow rose above the funnels of the engines; on many parts of the line the telegraph poles were buried up to their summits. No trains were able to come through; the last to attempt it got no farther than Leadburn, and was with difficulty run back to Edinburgh. For three days Peebles was completely cut off from the outside world. The telegraph wires had broken down from the weight of snow lying upon them, and from the pressure of the hurricane; no messages could be sent. There were no letters; no newspapers. The town might have been a dwelling-place of the dead. The streets were deserted; the houses barricaded by the snow, which also veiled the windows. The howling wind sang the dirge of the shrouded burgh.

Next day the weather improved, and snow ceased to fall. The railway snow-ploughs had therefore some chance to clear the line without its being filled up immediately. Day and night the work went on; and by noon on the following day the line was cleared.

That afternoon the first train got through as far as Peebles—no farther—with the mails, newspapers, and news of the outside world. What a relief passed over the burghers! Then only could one realize the conveniences of modern civilization, and the discomfort and alarm caused by their absence.

For these three days all communication had been cut off from our isolated town. Many strangers were storm-stayed, among them those who had come to attend the abandoned Fair. The Fiars Court had just been held in this the County Town; the jurors were unable to return to their homes.

All things considered, it was fortunate that no accident occurred, and that no lives were lost.

In the train which was unable to reach Peebles when the storm was at its height was a tonsilotome which I had wired for in order to excise the tonsils of a young woman. These were dangerously hypertrophied, threatening her with suffocation, not merely from bulk and pressure on the windpipe, but on account of the spasmodic closures of the glottis which the irritation caused. We managed to keep her alive while the block on the line continued; and when at last the train, with its four engines and four carriages, won through, I was

on the platform to meet it, and hurrying to the house of
the distressed damsel soon laid her tonsils at her feet!
The success of this operation brought the new doctor
into notice, and for long I enjoyed the reputation of a
specialist on tonsilotomy!

Next day this patient returned to her home in a
distant part of the county, and I did not see her again.
Recently, however, a middle-aged woman entered my
consulting-room, accompanied by three children; she
was a stout, fresh-coloured, and buxom matron. She
smilingly inquired whether I knew her; then informed
me that she was my erstwhile pallid, emaciated,
delicate patient of the historic storm.

There was of course during this time great distress
among masons, labourers, and allied trades, on account
of the prolonged winter. A soup-kitchen was opened,
and other beneficent agencies started, among them
being Saturday-evening entertainments on behalf of the
poor, at several of which I presided.

About this time, especially during such seasons of
distress, I began to gain first-hand knowledge of one of
the prime causes of disease, poverty, and crime in our
midst—namely, excessive drinking. How many of these
broken lives does a doctor encounter in the course of his
career! I have many a time seen officers and professional men tramping the roads as "gangrel bodies."
One schoolmaster, who had been head of a large college
abroad, I had to transfer from the poorhouse to the
asylum. Another who had been a practising physician
took the self-same road. In the lodging-houses in the
Long Close I have met hawkers, balloon-sellers, and
others, formerly men of culture and education, who
had fallen on evil days through drink. This curse
presents many cognate problems. Should a kirk-
session, for example, give coals and money to the wives
and children of these drunkards, knowing full well that
their generosity is merely supplying the father with

more money to spend on drink? My own view on this question is that the wives and children have enough to thole in blows, starvation, cold, oaths, and discomfort, without being outcasts from the love and beneficence of their fellows. Many of these families struggle bravely on against heavy odds, and deserve all the assistance they can get to help them in the battle.

The new church of Peebles was now approaching completion; and the subject of pews, sittings, and "bottom-rooms" was being hotly debated. The Magistrates were bent on seeing to what they considered to be their rights; so also were the Guildry and the Hammermen. Then the private heritors and farmers all required allocation in the new church, as did those who had possessed seats in the old one.

In former days a great abuse had crept into this matter of seats; those who possessed them had sold or bequeathed them to others, the result being that many of the pews belonged to members of other churches, who never occupied them, but drew rents from their tenants, which they applied to purposes purely secular. The Guildry and Hammermen even met once a year at a supper, and ate and drank the proceeds of their sittings! Members of the U.P. and Free Churches drew rents from the Old Church, which all the time they were bent on disestablishing and disendowing.

For many years this anomalous state of affairs continued in the case of my own pew, for which I paid the sum of twenty-five shillings yearly. One pound of this rejoiced the heart of a member of the U.P. congregation, while a pillar of the Free Kirk received half-a-crown; the remaining half-crown was all that accrued to the Auld Kirk.

Later, the kirk-session attempted to adjust these anomalies by requesting all seat-holders to allow the pews to be free and unappropriated at the evening services. This was an improvement, and made a first step towards the ideal condition of free pews for all who desire to attend Divine Service.

In the evenings at this time I read and studied much. Chambers' *History of Peeblesshire* interested me deeply, and inspired me to delve deep into Border history and tradition, among which my lines were now cast, and which were destined to become so intimate and integral a part of my own life. I also read at this time a *Life of George Eliot*, whose novels I admired sufficiently to recommend them as a course of reading to my mother, a severe and fastidious critic. Thackeray's *Pendennis*, too, held me engrossed by its able delineation of character; and Scott's *Fortunes of Nigel* whiled away many a solitary hour. I well remember regretting the absence among my acquaintance at that time of any "read men" with whom I could discuss bookish matters; and the resolve I then made to be content with the philosophic outlook, "my mind to me a kingdom is," even though I were compelled to range my unseen realm alone.

As a diversion, one winter evening, I celebrated the safe entry into the world of my seventh non-paying Peebles infant by an irreverent parody of Wordsworth, intended for the amusement of my mother. One or two verses of this youthful effort have survived the predatory years:

> I asked the eldest babe to tell
>   Their number? "Seven," said she,
> "And though we all in Peebles dwell,
>   Not one has paid your fee."
>
> "Then if of measles you should die,
>   Think you you'll win to Heaven?
> Non-payers don't go there," said I,
>   "No; out you'll stay, all seven."
>
> "None of us wanted to be born,"
>   The saucy maid replied,
> "Just send us back," she laughed in scorn,
>   "If you're not satisfied!"

"Non-paying babes," I frowning said,
"Can never be forgiven!"
'Twas throwing words away, for still
She mocked me with her laughter shrill,

"A bachelor like you, Sir, will
   Get no more than us seven!
So better burn your unpaid bill,
   And seek reward in Heaven!"

Towards the end of the year 1886 it had been announced to me that, if matters could be so arranged, Dr Fergusson would not be averse to our becoming partners as medical men in Peebles. We therefore met at dinner in his house and arranged preliminaries. Those of his patients whom he consulted expressed satisfaction and approval, the new arrangement tending to relieve many difficulties.

On 31st January I lectured in the Chambers Hall on "Monastic Life, Mediæval and Modern." I had made a special study of the subject in connection with the Fifeshire Abbey of Lindores. The hall was crowded, among the audience being the two medical men senior to me in the town. The night was wild and stormy; and Dr Fergusson, coming in late and drenched through, sat in his wet clothes till the proceedings ended. Immediately after the lecture he and I adjourned to a lawyer's office, and there signed our articles of co-partnery, for the purpose of which I was obliged to borrow the necessary money. We were now partners in name and in law; but alas! never in any other respect. For tragedy intervened, and he was actually my first patient under the co-partnery.

That very night he became ill, having contracted a chill while in an overworked and run-down condition. He rapidly grew worse; I called in another local doctor, also two Edinburgh specialists.

I sat up with him at nights, and between us we did everything humanly possible to save him. But he steadily worsened, and in a fortnight the end came.

Dr Fergusson had a warm, genial disposition, and was always ready with a kindly word or a hearty jest. He was a cool and skilful operator; and this added to the poignant sadness of the fact that he passed when in his prime, aged only forty-three, leaving a widow and eight children.

For some days before his funeral, the town had been placarded with bills announcing that Brigadier-General Wolfe-Murray of Cringletie would read selections from his Jubilee Diary at a public meeting. The General, with his picturesque bearing, eccentric manners, and racy, humorous conversation, had long been a familiar figure in Peeblesshire; any festive gathering addressed by him was assured of a merry time. As events turned out, the date advertised for his reading was the very day of the public funeral of Dr Fergusson. What was to be done? Lord Elibank, who was then being attended by me, asked my advice in the matter; we agreed that he should try to persuade the General that in the circumstances a humorous address, delivered in public, would be out of place, and should therefore be abandoned. The gallant officer, replying, made his own terms—namely, that Lord Elibank should attend at Cringletie in full naval uniform, complete with cocked hat and sword; and that the oration should be delivered there, to an audience of neighbours and friends, the General himself wearing full uniform also, as an officer of the Royal Archers. Lord Elibank duly complied; the address—a witty and entertaining affair—was delivered; public decorum and military prestige were alike satisfied; so all ended becomingly.

Nearly two years before this date, the Old Church of Peebles had been closed for public worship.

The fine new church was now (March 1887) ready

for opening and inauguration, and no one can deny that it occupies a singularly imposing and suitable position in the town at the head of the High Street, on the site of the ancient Castle of Peebles.

Originally in this church a straight wall extended right across the chancel, rising to the capitals of the pillars on either side. This wall supported a roof, above which it was proposed to place the choir and organ; underneath was to be the vestry and pres-bytery hall. This ugly arrangement converted the interior of the church into a square box; the choristers, when perched away up close to the rafters of the proposed roof, would present the appearance of caged birds.

No sooner was the wall erected than it was apparent that the interior effect of the church was in danger of being utterly spoilt, whereupon the committee had the good sense to demolish the wall which, like the renowned Balbus of the *Latin Grammar*, it had laboriously (though too impetuously) built.

The first couple "proclaimed" in the new church on the opening Sunday were—Clement Bryce Gunn, M.D., and Margaret Cameron, of the parish of Newburgh-on-Tay. Seated in my pew, I, as pro-spective bridegroom, heard our proclamation made, and duly received congratulations as the kirk "skailed." It had been thought advisable, in order to help my professional career at this stage, that we should be married without further delay.

At that time proclamations of banns were made twice in the morning and once in the evening; an improvement on the older fashion of announcing them on three successive Sundays. I remember a young couple, strangers living temporarily in the town, who were duly proclaimed one Sunday morning. The would-be Benedict was present, as I had been; but to his dismay and agitation, being ignorant of local

72

custom, he heard the banns proclaimed twice only, and not for the statutory third time. Scarcely waiting till the benediction was pronounced, he rushed wildly into the vestry and implored the minister, while yet two or three were gathered together in the fast-emptying church, to repair the fatal omission in the nick of time. "Come back to-night, and you'll hear the job completed!" he was reassured; and, in the hope that "all's well that ends well," he calmed down and went his ways.

Our marriage took place on 31st March 1887, at Cullalo House, Newburgh; my two brothers, the ministers of Stichill and Oxnam, assisting in the ceremony. On the following Saturday evening, one week after the proclamation of the banns, I brought my bride to her new home. Well do I remember driving her from the station in my newly acquired dog-cart, I holding the reins, she on the box-seat beside me, and the groom perched behind, through the streets of Peebles towards the Neidpath road, encountering many a friendly glance and smile directed at the young bride. On the threshold, when we reached it, stood my mother, ready with the traditional oatmeal cake sacred to a Scottish bridal, which she broke over the head of the bride as she set foot in her new home.

Poetry and prose, as so often in a doctor's life, were duly mingled even in those golden moments; for no sooner had I thus proudly domiciled my bride, than a reluctant glance at the slate revealed half-a-dozen summonses awaiting attention. Committing my wife to my mother's care with all the solicitude proper to the occasion, I forthwith set out on my appointed round, and merged the bridegroom in the practitioner with what philosophy I could muster.

FOR the next year or two, my life resembled that of the character in the Book of Job, "going up and down and to and fro," making and consolidating the practice. All was new to me in the countryside of Peeblesshire, and though the open-air driving was a severe trial in winter, and by night, the pleasure it afforded in fine weather made ample amends. The coachman whom I had inherited from my late partner, an old Ayrshire-man of Irish descent named Hanvey, proved an unfailing source of amusement, from his quaint and original outlook. One day, as we drove along a peculiarly muddy lane into which the wheels sank ominously deep, I noticed that he raised his hat impressively for a second, then replaced it very cautiously so that the brim reposed lightly on his hair. To my interested inquiry he responded solemnly: "When we sink through the glaur, sir, they'll ken where to dig, when they see my hat floating on the top!"

On one occasion (so Dr Fergusson had told me) he greeted him on his return to the house with a shilling, displayed with an air of proud satisfaction. "What's this?" asked the doctor. "A callan' cam' in frae the kintra wi' the toothache. Oh, it was sair! He waited a whilie for ye, an' it aye grew the sairer; so says he, 'I'm awa' to anither doctor!' But nae fears! I juist took the nippers ye gi'ed me for the bolts o' the carriage, an' pu'ed it oot afore he could stop me—so there's your shilling, sir!"

About the time of my marriage he encouraged me by the philosophic remark, delivered in lugubrious tones while cleaning the harness: "Ye may think, sir, ye hae a' the cares o' the warld on your shoulders the noo; but they're a' naething to the cares o' the meal-poke ance ye're mairr'et!"

Once only did Hanvey have an accident, when he allowed the mare to bolt down a long avenue at full gallop, through the gates and over a hedge. The carriage was left upturned on top of the hedge (ourselves beneath), while the mare careered round an adjacent field between the broken shafts. Fortunately no serious injury was done to life or limb, though the carriage suffered severely.

In 1888 our eldest child, Winifred Eleanor, was born. To the alarm and horror of the "old wives" of the neighbourhood, the infant was taken out on the following day in a heavy snowstorm; many were the prophecies of disaster, sure to attend on such a rash proceeding. Our first-born, nevertheless, has remained hardy and healthy ever since.

During these years I gave several courses of lectures on various subjects, medical and otherwise. One of these was a botanical series delivered to local mill-girls, whose interest in the structure and life-history of flowers surprised me greatly. Many of these girls became extremely skilful in dissecting and classifying specimens of plant life. Another course of addresses was delivered to the wives of working men, and dealt with their own health and that of their children. This was I think the most successful course ever undertaken by me; admission was free, and the attendance averaged a hundred and fifty each night. When the lectures ended I was the richer by a present of medical books made to me by the members, and by the certainty that many homes and families would benefit from the wider knowledge of health problems and precautions thus gained by the mothers.

At this time, in the new Parish Church, a bloodless

battle was taking place between the old order and the new. As the service gradually developed on altered lines, the number of boy-choristers in Eton jackets and wide white collars increased, and now threatened to oust completely the female singers, who had for many years reigned supreme. At length only one courageous lady, like Casabianca, stood her ground, when all around had fled; for several Sundays she alone represented what once had been a mixed choir, her singing sisterhood having been gently but relentlessly displaced by the encroaching masculine tide. But the day came when even her Stoic valour could cling no longer to a forlorn hope; she vanished, and the song-men and singing-boys carried all before them.

The death of Queen Victoria's son-in-law, the Emperor Frederick III. of Germany, after a brief and tragic reign of a hundred days, occurred at this time. His passing deeply impressed the public, who had followed the daily bulletins from the sickroom with affection and sorrow, and had learned from his gallant, unselfish bearing how a brave man can thole pain. Such lives are not spent in vain; nor is their end untimely, if through them the world learns something of the patience and fortitude of the human soul.

An interesting patient of mine at this time was old William Hogg, of Stobo Hope, whose father, an elder brother of the Ettrick Shepherd, had also been in his day a writer and something of a poet. Like his famous uncle, old William was rich in racial humour, having a cultured mind, brimful of anecdote and legend. Many a time he would recount to me some vivid tale of bygone days—among others, "how they brought the good news" of the victory of Waterloo to Tweedsmuir. His father was among those who ran out to greet the mail-coach (gaily decorated for the occasion with flags and streamers), and shared in the tumultuous outburst of excitement created by the news.

The inhabitants of Peebles enjoyed an excitement of another kind, in the shape of an earthquake shock which occurred early in 1889. Having sifted and examined the many conflicting accounts of the occurrence volunteered by my Peebles patients as I went my rounds, I undertook to verify and supplement these by information from Peeblesshire farmers and others in outlying districts—a kind of amateur seismological survey. This data was later embodied, by an eminent seismologist of Birmingham, in a paper which was read before the Royal Society.

About this time occurred an annual local "diversion" —namely, the visit of Bostock's Menagerie, which took up its accustomed stance by the riverside. Late one Saturday night, when the week's performances had come to an end, I was summoned to attend a patient in one of the caravans. All was bustle and confusion on the showground; the camp-fires glowed redly, and the booths, lit by naphtha-flares, were being hastily dismantled for the midnight journey. The lions and tigers, still excited by the rolling of the drums, roared vehemently from their cages; the caravans shook in the darkness with the sound. I found my patient in a large wagon: a fine young woman with long beautiful hair streaming across her pillows. She was, it seemed, the lion-tamer's wife. As she was in agony, and an immediate operation was essential, I lost no time, but, having administered chloroform, operated there and then. In that swaying wagon, with the swinging oil-lamp yielding an uncertain flicker of light, the task was not easy; I did all I could, and hoped for the best. Long before daybreak the whole encampment had folded their tents like the Arabs, and as silently stolen away.

Often, in the months that followed, did I recall that strange midnight scene, with its bizarre setting, and speculate upon the fate of my unusual patient. On

Christmas Eve arrived a parcel containing, among other gifts, a doll for Winifred; and a grateful letter from the lion-tamer, assuring me of the complete success of the operation on his now healthy and happy young wife. For many years afterwards, when from time to time Bostock's Circus revisited Peebles, tickets were duly sent to us for the performance, and thereafter, having paid a state call upon Mrs Bostock in her caravan, we visited my erstwhile patient in the lion-tamer's wagon, and her children exchanged greetings with my own.

In autumn 1889 all Scotland was shocked and saddened by news of what was long known as "the Mauricewood Pit disaster." This occurred near Penicuik, Midlothian, where a raging fire broke out at the bottom of a large coal-pit, and between sixty and seventy miners lost their lives. Forty families were thus suddenly deprived of their bread-winners; the misery and distress of acute poverty aggravated the bitterness of bereavement.

One of those who laboured night and day with tireless energy, both in heartening the stricken families and in raising relief funds, was S. R. Crockett, then minister of the Free Church at Penicuik. Subscriptions flowed in from all parts of Scotland, for the tragedy had saddened the whole Border country, and sympathy spread far beyond local bounds. On the Sunday following the disaster, thousands of people attended the funerals of the victims. The coffins lay on the benches outside the church door: a grim and terrible array. Here and there a Boys' Brigade cap and belt marked the coffin of a young lad; the bride-to-be of one man, whose marriage was to have taken place on the very evening of the tragedy, now stood weeping by his open grave. It was not till seven months afterwards, when the flooded levels of the pit were at last pumped dry, and the search could be resumed in safety, that the last of the miners' bodies were brought to the surface, and buried near those of their comrades.

About this time there died at West Linton an arresting "character," the local practitioner, who might well have sat to R. L. Stevenson for one of his pen-portraits.

Andrew Bonthron, M.D., had been for a quarter of a century one of the most remarkable personages in the Borders; with his great square florid countenance, glossy jet-black hair curling over his shoulders, and oddly assorted costume of blue serge, worn with knickerbockers and leather leggings, he looked like a stage pirate. His habits were as eccentric as his appearance; he usually worked by night, visiting his patients in the small hours, and instead of going to bed slept, fully dressed, in a sitting position on two chairs. His oddities sprang not from self-conceit, but from a philosophic disregard of all conventions or customs, save those of comfort and convenience. It was said that in his later years he sought solace in opium; and I have myself seen him fall sound asleep between the actions of striking a match and lighting his pipe. But he was a man of marked ability, confidence, and resource. His patients, as I had occasion to discover, relied on him implicitly, and with reason, for both in practice and therapeutics he ever went straight to the mark.

Once or twice I met him in consultation, and was struck, as was everyone who knew him, by his unique character and personality. He had a wonderful gentleness and serenity when attending a patient, so much so that even those not destined to recover felt the better for his cheery word and kindly philosophy. He was insatiably interested in everything under the sun, from ploughing-matches to balloon-flights; all was grist that came to his philosophic mill. At the Edinburgh Forestry Exhibition he was observed preparing to make an ascent in the great balloon, by a Border acquaintance, who cried out in alarm: "Come back, man! Remember your patients!" A sardonic chuckle was the only response; the giant balloon, with its intrepid passenger aboard, sailed gaily away, and ultimately landed the doctor, not, as his friend had feared, in Kingdom Come, but in some part of the Kingdom of Fife.

About the beginning of 1890 the complaint which we now call "Influenza" had begun to appear in the district. It was quite a new malady to this generation, though perfectly known and recognized by our grandparents. In former days whole ships' crews were frequently and suddenly laid low by this mysterious infection, not a single able-bodied seaman being left to navigate the ship.

At first in this neighbourhood people were inclined to make light of the "Russian Influenza," or *la grippe*, as it was called. But too soon its serious nature made itself manifest in the profound prostration of its victims, with high temperatures, complications, head affections, and other dangerous neuroses accompanying or following in its train. Many a strong man attempted to throw off the disease, only to be cut off in his prime by the severity of the influenza itself, or by the fatal pneumonia which so often supervened. Soon it began to be greatly dreaded, and, as frequently happens, those who were most afraid of the infection were therefore prone to suffer from it in a severe form. This acute dread has a depressing effect upon the powers of resistance of its possessors. Since that year we have been regularly visited by this scourge. Its variety is one of its most striking manifestations. One year will bring a nervous type of the malady; another an abdominal; a third, a crop of bronchial and pulmonary cases, and so on.

I well remember the first three cases I saw; all

occurred on the same day. The first was at a neighbouring farm, where the farmer's wife lay prostrate
from *la grippe*. I had never seen a case, but told her
that from my reading I should diagnose it as this new
and painful malady. Immediately thereafter I was
called to another woman in the same condition; and
later in the day to a man, in agony from the same cause.
Since that day their name has been legion, and the
ranks of the suffering army have grown yearly.

It was now my lot to experience a new phase of the
illness; this time a cerebral type. During the night my
bell rang: a summons from an outlying farm. It was
a frosty night, starry and clear; the ground lightly
powdered with hoar-frost. As there was no accessible
driving-road I had some considerable distance to walk,
over hill-slopes riddled with morasses and bogs.
Suddenly, as I plodded on my solitary way, there darted
past me without a sound a flying figure in white, which
vanished like a wraith among the adjacent hillocks,
leaving no trace behind. Surely an authentic ghost at
last: the first of my medical career! Sorely perplexed
in mind, I made my way towards the remote cottage
from which the summons had come, and was met by
the shepherd who occupied it, with the alarmed cry:
"Hae ye seen Johnnie, Doctor? He's awa' to the hill!"
A sudden influenza seizure had caused delirium;
Johnnie, the patient, had been locked in his room,
pending my arrival, but had escaped by the window,
and in desperation taken to the hill. An exciting midnight chase ensued, the shepherd and I scouring the
hill-slopes in all directions; finally we ran the sweating,
shivering "ghost" to earth, captured and brought him
home. Somewhat to my surprise, the lad was little the
worse of his night adventure, and made a rapid
recovery. So vanished for ever my most promising
spectre, exposed as a mere caprice of the influenza
fiend!

For some time I had been passing through that regular course of "Burns fever" which every true Scot must sooner or later thole. As Vice-President of the local Burns Club, I did what I could to impart a literary and educational flavour to the annual proceedings on 25th January, which at that epoch were more concerned with whisky and haggis than with a just appreciation of the poet's genius. I therefore organized Burns competitions throughout the schools, and the young candidates competed publicly for prizes awarded for reciting Burns' lyrics or for singing his songs. The scheme—a novel one in those days—not only stimulated interest in literature and brought many new and thoughtful members to the Burns Club, but was of interest as showing what the youth of Scotland could achieve by the study of our great vernacular poet.

An odd circumstance, undetected at the time, caused one of our Burns suppers to linger long in the memory of those present. It was held in one of the local hotels, and I was acting as croupier. A message arrived from the landlord asking whether we would allow two visitors who were staying at the hotel to join our party. We duly consented, and two quiet, unobtrusive men entered, were made welcome, took their places at the festive board, and joined in the conversation throughout the evening. The strangers appeared to be middle-class tradesmen of good position. No introductions were made; the spirit of "a man's a man for a' that" prevailed; the evening passed off pleasantly and decorously enough.

Later, however, we learned to our horror that one of our unknown guests had been none other than the notorious murderer Deeming! In an isolated house near Manchester, to which he had conveyed his wife and several children, he had murdered them all, burying the bodies of his victims in a grave dug beneath the kitchen floor, which he had then carefully cemented to avoid discovery. He succeeded in escaping to Australia, but was eventually arrested, tried, and executed. It gave one something of a shudder to realize that this was the same man with whom we had passed an evening of fellowship, and who had joined hands with us in singing *Should Auld Acquaintance be forgot*! This chance acquaintance of a night was not soon forgotten, at all events, but invested the memory of that particular "Burns Nicht" with the lurid light of tragic drama.

Among recollections of public happenings in the year 1890, the opening of the newly completed Forth Bridge stands out clearly. During a violent hurricane, in early March of that year, the Prince of Wales drove in the last rivet; and the gigantic structure, with its two enormous spans each measuring 1710 feet, and the many lesser arches which flanked them on either side, stood complete. Seven years of labour had gone to its construction; but the result amply rewarded those master-minds responsible for the inception of its vast and complicated design.

An interesting link with the past was severed about this time by the death of John Stirling, an ex-Provost of Peebles. This octogenarian scholar was equally devoted to his garden and to the Greek and Latin authors; he would quote Tacitus and Horace as he bent above his plants, and was as familiar with the Greek Testament as with the Scottish Psalter. His memory was prodigious, and his society keenly relished by the professoriate of Edinburgh and Glasgow universities. He could remember the dinner given to Sir Walter Scott in the Cross Keys Inn at Peebles, and that other festive evening in the Tontine Hotel, where "Christopher North" (Professor Wilson) was the guest of honour.

In June of this year (1890) our first son was born.

The day was warm and sunny, and we decorated the bed with pendent boughs of hawthorn, which filled the air with fragrance, and covered the quilt with its petals. According to the custom in the Clan Gunn, by which the eldest son is always named George (originally after George Gunn the Crowner, of the sixteenth century), we called our eldest son by this name, which had been my father's and my eldest brother's also. He was baptized at the annual open-air service at St Gordian's Cross, in Manor, on the spot which tradition has hallowed as the meeting-place of Roman legionaries for Christian worship. The sunlit hills and green pastures of Manor provide a perfect setting for this annual pilgrimage. The countless associations woven by history, legend, and tradition round every landmark bring the sense of the past, with all its wonder and romance, very close to the mind. From all directions the great crowd of pilgrims approaches the ancient site; many use the old drove-roads, now solitary grass tracks, which link the quiet valley with its neighbours beyond the hills. Never do our ancient Scottish Psalm tunes sound more impressive than when they rise in the still air, memories of Covenanting times echoing in their sound. Nor is the appropriate message of such words as "I to the hills will lift mine eyes," or the pastoral imagery of the 23rd Psalm, lost upon the modern mind as the worshippers stand there. It is an occasion when the generations of men meet and touch in a continuity of spirit; when the dead inspire the living, and the past breathes its benediction upon the present. In my mind on that summer Sunday, as I stood on the green hillside before the congregation, to present my infant son for entrance into the Church of his fathers, gathered many thoughts. These, in after days, crystallized into a sonnet on the annual pilgrimage, a few lines from which I append here:

A congregation of forgotten dead
Beneath the press of living feet sleeps well;
We feel their souls in touch with matins said,
With old-world melody and Scripture read;
And thus the continuity is kept:—
The Church and Service live though years have fled
And fabric fall, and naught save mounds wind-swept
Its site enshrine.   The Spirit breathes on every age,
And unborn feet keep up the ancient Pilgrimage.

During this year I was moved to investigate the curious earthwork, cruciform in shape, which lends a special interest to one of the Meldon Hills near Peebles. This great Cross measures 144 feet in every direction, and has boundaries of turf, eight feet broad, rising from one to three feet above the surrounding ground. The summit above it is surrounded by an entrenchment of earth and stones; and at some distance beneath it are traces of what may—or may not—have been a crescentic prehistoric village. Close to the vast Cross run many of the great drove-roads, once the main arteries of transport for the sheep and cattle of these Border regions. Many an eminent antiquarian have I conducted to the spot, and many and various have been the learned theories advanced as to the genesis and history of the Cross. No perfectly satisfactory hypothesis, however, has been established on these points; the Meldon, or Hill of Fire, still hides the secret of the Cross within its heart. One practical result, however, issued from my investigations: I induced the Ordnance Survey authorities to include the cruciform area in their official maps of the neighbourhood, so that, though still unexplained, the curious phenomenon is no longer unrecorded or ignored.

One of my long-distance journeys about this time took me as far afield as Lamington; the latter part of the journey had perforce to be made on foot. I had left Tweed behind me, and now approached the River

Clyde, on the other side of which lay my patient's house. The river was in full flood; no bridge was visible. I hailed a countryman with the inquiry: "How can I get across the water?" "On stilts, man; we a' gang on stilts here!" was the laconic reply. Discouraged, I sat down on the river bank to consider "The Doctor's Dilemma." No stilts were available, and even had they been I had grave fears that the acrobatic performance of fording a raging torrent with their aid was beyond me. Presently my gloomy meditations were interrupted by the rumble of approaching wheels: a farm-cart loaded with turnips. I at once hailed the carter: "Will you take me across?" "Hae ye no' got stilts?" was his counter-question. When satisfied that I had none about me, he allowed me to mount the cart on top of the turnips, with the sinister remark: "Mind, it's yer ain risk, no' mine's!" Precariously balanced on top of the turnip-load, I clung on for dear life as the cart plunged midstream in the torrent. But though turnips fell freely as we proceeded, we negotiated both outward and homeward voyages without mishap; and during the journey back to Peebles by train, I pondered the advisability of adding a pair of stilts to my professional equipment, for future eventualities of a similar kind.

An incident of extreme medical interest, unique in my experience, occurred about this time in my practice. I was driving to an urgent maternity case some distance away, when I encountered a gig coming from the opposite direction, driven at a furious pace. Its driver at once pulled up, and signed to my man to do likewise. "We're juist seeking you, Doctor!" shouted the new-comer; "Tam here has got his airm aff i' the threshing-mill!" "His arm off! Surely not!" I ejaculated, with a hasty glance at the lad of fifteen sitting beside him, wrapped in a shepherd's plaid. To my amazement the boy shouted indignantly: "'No aff,' dae ye say? I'll sune show ye! Here it's!'"—and with that he held up in one hand his other arm, completely severed close to the shoulder, and brandished it in our faces. Never shall I forget the look of stupefaction on my coachman's face at the gruesome sight of those cold contracted fingers, emerging from the torn shirt and sleeve.

What was to be done? I could not endanger two lives by neglecting the maternity case which awaited me; yet here was another human being, young and courageous, in the gravest straits. I bade them drive on to Peebles and call in another doctor; and promising to return as soon as possible, hastened on with all speed. All went well with mother and child, and in less time than I had ventured to hope for, I was amputating Tom's splintered bone at the shoulder-joint, a fellow-practitioner having administered the anæsthetic. After two hours' rest we had the lad conveyed home in a cab, surrounded by hot bottles; early next day I drove out to visit him, filled with apprehension lest the combined effects of shock, exposure, and delay should have ended in a fatal collapse during the night. The first object which met my eyes on entering the farm-house was the redoubtable Tom, sitting up and supping a big bowl of porridge with every appearance of satisfaction! The wound healed rapidly, and in a short time the lad was up and out-of-doors again, wrapped in his plaid, laughing and joking as usual. The incident had a touch of the macabre about it, however, which even the astonishing stoicism of its hero could not entirely banish from the mind.

At the close of 1890 and during the early weeks of 1891, life was complicated by a railway strike involving practically the whole rail-transport system of the country. The strikers chose their time wisely, aware that the disorganization of Christmas traffic was the best means of bringing their demands forcibly before the attention of the country.

No warning was given; the men demanded a ten-hours day, and ceased work until the point should be conceded. Public opinion, on the whole, sympathized with the workers' grievances, which were generally felt to be just; as a result, the irritation and inconvenience of the strike were on the whole borne with considerable patience.

The strike continued for six weeks, during which time there was little or no intercourse between separate parts of the kingdom. Newspapers and mails became irregular, and in many places ceased altogether.

At the Waverley Station, passengers would sit hopefully for hours in stationary trains, uncertain as to when, if ever, an engine would be forthcoming. Now and then a train would start off in gallant style, manned by railway pensioners and other veterans of the company, who had not joined forces with the strikers; only to come ignominiously to a dead stop in the midst of a tunnel, where it would remain immobile in the darkness for hours. Hungry children and delicate women endured the long delays as best they might; wintry weather and short dark January days added to the general discomfort.

At length the men agreed to resume duty; the railway companies formulated schemes for shorter hours and better pay; and, to the relief of all concerned, the strike ended.

About this time a telephone exchange was installed in the town—an innovation regarded with wondering interest, mingled with characteristic caution, by the inhabitants. I was the first person to join it, and for about a year remained the sole subscriber, with the exception of the chemist to whom I telephoned prescriptions. The charm of telephonic communication in such circumstances soon palls; I decided that the game, in such restricted conditions, was not worth the candle, so abandoned the exchange in favour of a private wire to the chemist.

Time passed; the adamantine reluctance of the Peebles public to patronize the new invention melted away by slow degrees; so that eventually I was emboldened to rejoin the exchange, and my professional *tête-à-tête* with the chemist was extended to a wider sphere of usefulness.

Similarly, when that "new-fangled" invention, the automobile, was introduced, I was the first person in the county to use one. One or two Border newspapers commented, amusingly enough, on the anomaly of such pioneer proceedings on the part of an antiquarian enthusiast, who might be expected to ignore progress while clinging, limpet-like, to the vanished past. But I have always striven as far as possible to keep the mind alert and sensitive to conditions new as well as old, and to avoid the aridities of Dr Dry-as-dust *et hoc genus omne*. One may study and absorb the poetry of the past, which illumines every standing-stone, every quern, every ancient cross or other relic of a bygone age, with a beauty and a dignity of its own. But unless the mind be kept fresh and alert to learn the lessons which these survivals teach, and to apply them to modern life, the study of archæology is indeed a useless business. Nevertheless, a dash of ecclesiasticism in my composition leads me to uphold the remembrance and observance of old customs, anniversaries and traditions, both in the family circle and beyond it. At this time we regularly celebrated among others the feasts of Hallowe'en, St Valentine, and Candlemas Eve; the last-named (1st February) according to the advice given by Herrick:

> Down with rosemary and so
> Down with the bay and mistletoe:

That so the superstitious find
No one least branch there left behind.
For look, how many leaves there be
Neglected there—maids, trust to me,
So many goblins ye shall see!

Occasionally a few hardy evergreen sprays would continue to decorate our rooms after 2nd February had dawned, and the household was compelled to risk the goblins, my warnings notwithstanding.

Our Hallowe'en celebrations, with the traditional accompaniments of a great tub of apples to be "ducked" for, and plenty of nuts and fruit, were always hilariously enjoyed by the children.

On my rounds one Hallowe'en I had occasion to visit a very poor home, and to my surprise found that the Eve of All Hallows was being duly observed there, as by my own fireside: with this difference, that the tub of dirty water on the floor, round which half-a-dozen all-but-naked children were gathered in semi-darkness, shouting and singing, contained ONE APPLE! The contrast between this crowded, ill-lit hovel, haunted by poverty and disease, and the bright scene of revelry I had just left at home, was eloquent indeed. Yet these street Arabs were for the moment carefree, oblivious of time, making revel with their single apple as happily as princes. Later, I embodied the incident in a sonnet, *Hallowe'en*.

Now, too, as 14th February approached, I noted with regret the complete disappearance of valentines from the shops; not one could be procured for love or money. A few years ago one saw them everywhere; but the saint of lovers has apparently gone out of fashion. In contrast to the soft, flimsy tracery of the valentine, with its border of lace and its garland of spring flowers, we have the hardness and sleekness of its rival and supplanter, the Christmas card. I regret the change; the secret hunt for *the* appropriate valentine, duly drenched in sentiment and smothered in lace, holds happy memories of courting days and youthful visions.

The last notable Border event of the year 1891 was the great flood—the highest in the memory of man—which occurred on 21st September. Three days of northerly gales and torrential rain preceded the flood itself. At midnight on the 20th, I was summoned to Stobo Hope Head—my wildest and most inaccessible country journey, dangerous in all weathers. The storm raged so furiously in the small hours that neither man nor beast could venture forth; but at dawn, despite misgivings, we set out with horse and trap. It was a wild dark journey; both rain and wind "against us furiously rose up in wrath"; but the good horse battled on, and after a four-hours struggle we came in sight of our goal: a solitary house standing far up the lonely valley. The case was an urgent one, entailing great suffering to the patient, which I was fortunate in being able to ease; so we were received with gratitude and relief.

On the homeward journey—made, mercifully, by daylight—we could perceive the havoc wrought by the storm during the long hours of that memorable night. Every burn was now a torrent; every road submerged. Tweed, Manor, and Lyne waters were foaming, surging seas of darkest amber. The floods, as they rushed along, bore down stacks, sheep, stooks, doors, bridges: a whirling medley of flotsam and jetsam.

We reached Peebles to find Tweedgreen completely flooded; the low-lying houses were invaded by the waters to the depth of two or three feet. All the wooden bridges in the district were swept away; the south piers of Tweed Bridge were undermined, and the old oak beams, on which its stone piers then rested, were exposed. (Since this flood, the "Tree Bridges" have been replaced by iron ones; and Tweed Bridge itself widened and strengthened.)

All rail transport was cut off, as many of the embankments had been undermined, and several alarming landslips occurred. It was an odd sight to see the signal-cabins standing solitary, like lighthouses, in the midst of wide watery wastes, while the adjacent rails were submerged, and the rushing water poured over, as well as under, the useless bridges.

Even the local gas-works was invaded by the flood, and but for a timely store of gas in a gasometer elsewhere in the town, Egyptian darkness would have been added to our other plagues. As it was, there was much distress and hardship for the poor in the flooded areas, and the kirk-session, at my suggestion, at once agreed to make a distribution of coals to enable these unfortunates to dry their houses and bedding.

The effects of this disastrous flood were long visible in the country-side, and to this day one may see many puzzling banks of gravel deposited on fields remote, to all appearance, from any river. These are the legacy of that wild September night when so many streams became torrents, burst their bounds in all directions, and invaded the surrounding country-side.

[IN January, 1892, Dr Gunn adopted the practice of keeping a Journal. Excerpts from this record, which was continued spasmodically for several years, now replace the autobiographical narrative.—ED.]

Jan. 31*st*, 1892.   To-day ends the first month of the new year—one month of my Journal!   I have not dared to make any solemn resolution anent this diary-keeping, lest I weary of it: but I would fain ensure two things: (1) that if I die young, my children may learn more of their father's doings than I did of mine, who died when I was six months old; and (2) that a hundred years hence others may read the daily adventures and varied thoughts of a country doctor of the nineteenth century.

Feb. 2*nd.*   At this season I have many cases of grave illness in the homes of the very poor.   Here, if anywhere, one encounters practical religion in its noblest form.   Night after night the same neighbour—often the only available helper—will sit tending a sick mother, or helping her with a dying child.   I am often struck by the look of patient expectancy which the face of the watcher assumes in these long vigils; irritation, fatigue, and impatience vanish completely, though one knows that the woman has her own troubles in the background.   Nor do these Samaritans look for thanks or reward: duty and religion are the motive forces.   All through my career, these quiet ministrations of the poor to the poor have deeply impressed and touched me.

Feb. 16*th.*   At nine in the morning I started in the trap, in a blinding snowstorm, to visit a cottage some miles up the Lyne Valley.   Four inches of snow had already fallen; the roads were heavy, and the landscape shrouded in a white pall, against which were

93

silhouetted the stark lines of the dykes and the black tracery of leafless trees. The sombre river reflected a leaden sky. All the way, as we drove through this silent world, snow fell ceaselessly, noiselessly; we grew stiff with cold, and purple of visage, as the horse plodded doggedly on. A diphtheria case awaited me at the cottage, where, under one roof, reside two parents, five children, one lodger, his mother, two cows, four collie dogs, three cats, and seventy hens! This assemblage is deeply indebted to the aseptic and antiseptic properties of bracing cold and fresh air, which they enjoy perforce in these solitudes, for the fact that there is not more disease and mortality among them.

March 1st. My spare time is occupied mainly with my wife and two bairns, and with reading. I hate to be idle, and am always healthiest in mind and body when fully occupied. I have been reading Marie Bashkirtseff's *Diary*: a complex medley, full of interest both as a psychological study and as a human document. She is neither to be envied nor emulated; yet "what's done we partly may compute, but know not what's resisted," in such cases, is a wise saying. By way of contrast, I turned to the *Journal* of Sir Walter Scott. Next to the Bible, this is a book which has influenced me in a pre-eminent degree. The elements of character which it contains—a nature honest, brave, hard-headed, solid, religious in the true though not in the formalist sense—make it a book to build upon. The manner, too, in which Scott the man reveals Scott the hero, at the downfall of all his hopes and ambitions, gives one courage and tenacity of purpose amid the storms of life.[1]

I have also just finished *The Little Minister*, a tale

[1] In 1932, Dr Gunn had the satisfaction of adding to his Scott bookshelf the published edition of his daughter Winifred's play, *Scott of Abbotsford*, and of witnessing its production in London, Edinburgh and Glasgow [ED.].

by J. M. Barrie. He has the gift of description, of delineating human nature with acute observation, and a shrewd eye for small things and "unconsidered trifles." This book has touches of philosophy, and plenty of satire to keep it tart. I find that though I do not grow to love any of his characters, their originality holds my interest and piques my curiosity to know more. I find reading a great refreshment, and visit my patients in a much more cheerful frame of mind when reinvigorated by contact with the books which interest me.

March 2nd. This has been a great tooth-pulling day. Dental cases abound at present, owing probably to the prevalence of bitter east winds blowing over snow: a cruel combination. Last night I struggled on foot through deep snow to a patient in Newbie Glen; in summer the place is beautiful, but at present bleak, bare, unfriendly, and all but inaccessible. It was a night of Cimmerian mirk; howling blasts of wind blew out the gig-lamps, which I carried in my hands so as not to miss the path. Consequently, on the return journey I had to creep as best I might in the darkness along a precipitous sheep-track overhanging a steep cliff, feeling for each step as I went. Presently I heard a shout from below—my coachman had come up in search of me; we rekindled one of the lamps, which this time withstood the gale, and regained the trap in safety. Country practice in Peeblesshire in summer can be delightful; but these winters are truly terrible. Snowstorms, blizzards, journeyings, fastings, long solitary vigils, and above all, the intense cold—these things tend to age one's frame and to intensify any physical weakness one may possess. I should not wish, if the choice were given me, to die in summer, when all is green, joyous, and pleasant; in winter one's regrets would be fewer.[1]

[1] Dr Gunn died on Christmas Day, 1933 [ED.].

May 27*th*. Three incidents have made me laugh to-day: the laugh ironic, the laugh Byronic, and the laugh sardonic! Firstly, on visiting an elderly patient who has suffered acutely for many years from a form of *tic douloureux*, I found her overjoyed at the wonderfully beneficial effects of some pills which I had prescribed. They are composed entirely of bread. Like the patient in the Bible, she has suffered much from many physicians, among them myself; we have poured out the entire pharmacopœia upon her, and now, having exhausted its resources, we revert to *pil. mica panis*, with wonder-working results! This episode supplied me with the laugh ironic.

Secondly, the inevitable girl came to consult me as to the inevitable symptoms which, she declared, baffled all conjecture or investigation. When informed that she was merely about to become a mother, she flew into the usual frenzy of expostulation, denial, and furious indignation, directed solely at me and my unwelcome diagnosis. I tholed the storm of resentment philosophically, as a doctor learns to do; but when the door closed on her, protesting to the last, took refuge in the laugh Byronic as a solatium.

Thirdly, a woman whom I had attended in a severe and protracted nocturnal confinement, and to whom I had paid five subsequent visits, driving several miles each way, arrived to settle her account. One guinea —the sum in question—was extorted with the greatest difficulty on my part, and the maximum amount of reluctance on hers. No wonder that a country doctor seldom leaves a penny! Left alone with my hard-earned guinea, I enjoyed the laugh sardonic to the full.

May 31*st*. To-day I examined several volumes of the Burgh Records of this place, dating from the year 1590. I have some notion, at present not very clearly defined, of using this material as a basis for notes on Scottish Border life and customs in the olden times.

I find such ancient relics both touching and engrossing. One sees the continuity of human experience from one generation to another, and the unchanging characteristics of human nature. The hands which wrote those pages are long since dust; so, too, a hundred years hence, will my own hand be. And who knows? These pages of mine, the warp and woof of a doctor's daily life, may miss the luck of preservation, which the old civic records have had.

June 2nd, 1892. During the night I was summoned to a maternity case. As I left the house, the moon was rising; a silver radiance scintillated on the surface of Tweed as I crossed the bridge; the air, despite the season, was cool and frosty. In contrast to the silver moon-rays, the windows of the spinning-mill, with their yellow gas-lamps, shone garishly. A cold breeze rustled the foliage of the trees as I passed, banishing all traces of sleep from the brain. Often have I noted how clear the mental vision is by night. Faust's lines ring constantly in my head as I drive or walk on my night journeys:

> Hushed now the field, the meadow lies
> Beneath the veil of deepest night;
> And solemn thoughts within us rise
> Too holy for the garish light.
> Calm now the blood that wildly ran;
> Asleep the hand of lawless strife.
> Now wakes to life the love of man,
> The love of God now wakes to life.

Ever since my Newburgh days, when to ride long distances by night was a common experience, I have found the mental stimulus of these night expeditions far outweigh their attendant drawbacks. True, I have learned that the gratitude of nocturnal patients, perfervid enough in the small hours, melts like morning mists before the sunrise of ordinary daily existence! But I use these silent hours in the open air, when all is still and solitary, to make new plans, overturn old ones, suggest new methods and form new resolutions. At such times I see with clearest vision my shortcomings, faults, and errors. Remorse often visits me on these journeys; one's motives are illumined in a manner rarely possible by day, when all is bustle and confusion. Yet one reaches out towards the lofty hills, and the healing silence of the night, which lead one's thoughts away from the world towards God.

June 8th. This evening I made a tour of investigation of Neidpath Castle, accompanied by my wife and our four-year-old Winifred. It has been a day of great heat; scarcely a breath of wind stirred the leafy trees as we made our way towards the old keep. Hawthorn and lilac are flowering abundantly, and the laburnum, with its "dropping wells of fire," will be in full glory next week. The white, dusty roads are bestrewn with the stamens of the elms.

Having invaded the old Castle, we proceeded to pervade it from lowermost donjon to loftiest pinnacle. From the battlements the prospect resembled some mediæval fairyland of glamour and romance. To the south one saw the wooded hill whence Cromwell bombarded the Castle, with the silver links of Tweed winding silently below. At our feet lay grassy terraces, flecked with placidly browsing sheep and skipping lambs, and dotted with scampering rabbits; the ruined chapel and outbuildings of the fortress, and its avenue of emerald-green turf, guarded by immemorial yews, a white ribbon of roadway separating it from the ancient garden where fruit-trees flourished and blossomed in bygone days. In the near vista one descried Peebles Kirk, Mill, and Bridge; farther away, the slopes of Lea Pen and Shiel Kips. A cloudless sky, blue and serene; a westering sun; the murmur of doves and the call of a distant cuckoo, completed the magic spell. Winifred, with her bright hair curling about her ears in mediæval-saint fashion, seemed part of the picture.

In contrast to such surrounding beauty, the Castle itself, that rugged, dogged mass of masonry a thousand years old, loomed up grim and obdurate; we creatures of a day, viewing the scene, could only marvel. Such beauty cannot be painted in words; one can but feel it, finding "tongues in trees, books in the running brooks, sermons in stones, and good in everything."

August 20*th*. I have just left a sorrowful scene. An infant aged two years has been run over in the street by a cart, the wheel passing over the child's head. Hastily summoned, I found in a small cramped room the usual crowd of wailing women, and the child—mercifully unconscious—gasping out its life on a kindly neighbour's lap. Nothing could be done; I said a word of sympathy to the poor agonized mother, and left. It is strange and sad to realize that all her life she must henceforth associate my face and form with the tragedy of her baby's death.

Sudden deaths have been frequent hereabouts of late. One woman to whom I was called recently, I found lying dead on the floor of her kitchen, in the act of baking scones for her household. On the bake-board lay a circle of dough, rolled out and quartered; newly baked scones stood stacked in rows at the window. The girdle was on the fire, awaiting the next batch; and beside the woman lay a bunch of feathers with which she had been about to dust the girdle, and which had slipped from her dead hand. The stricken looks of her husband and son, who had left her apparently in good health an hour or two before, haunted me for hours. In such cases, even when death is evident at the first glance, one instinctively delays for a few seconds, making play with the stethoscope, examining the body and so forth, before pronouncing the fatal word: "Dead." Once said, there is no recall; and in these sudden cases the look of blank, incredulous horror, and the stunned bewilderment which succeeds it, is hard to encounter and hopeless to relieve.

Oct. 6*th*. Lord Tennyson died this morning at 1.35 A.M. The process was a slow, gradual sinking, consciousness remaining to the end; in his own words:

> Such a tide as moving seems asleep,
>   Too full for sound or foam,
> When that which drew from out the boundless deep
>   Turns again home.

Whether he was a great original poet or no, posterity will judge; he has certainly given pleasure and consolation to very many. His *In Memoriam* I think will live, for it plumbs the human heart and its most poignant sorrows; much of his other work seems shallow in comparison.

Oct. 21*st*. This morning brings the first approach of winter; snow was falling when I rose, and the hill-tops are clothed in white. The effects of the early morning frosts are visible in the roadways, plentifully strewn with fallen leaves. I note that the ash always falls early, not leaf by leaf, but at the junction of the leaf-stalk with the branch. It is odd, amid this wintry landscape, to see so much corn standing still uncut, not only on the high ground, but all over the county. The farmers have not been able to "win" it because of the recent rains. Late seasons are no modern curse, however, as I find in the Burgh Records of very early date, references to harvests delayed as late as this. Our farmers must thole it philosophically, in the spirit of the burgh motto, "*Contra nando incrementum.*"

Nov. 26*th*. Much interest is being aroused by the discovery of forgeries of the works of Burns and Scott, perpetrated by an Edinburgh druggist. Alleged authentic poems, letters, and autographs have, it seems, been circulated by him through the media of auction sales and dealers, and have been to some extent accepted as genuine by the public. An "autograph" letter by Burns, and a poem entitled "To a Rosebud," were the first of these impostures to arouse suspicion; their authenticity was impugned in the Press, and acrimonious correspondence ensued. The versatile druggist, undeterred, followed up his "discoveries" with "The Poor Man's Prayer," an alleged "new" and unpublished Burns fragment. It has now been discovered that this "find" appeared in the *London Magazine* of 1766, when Burns was seven years old!

The perpetrator of these wholesale forgeries has from the outset steadfastly declined to state the source of his "discoveries," or to submit them for inspection by the British Museum. All however is now exposed, and the pawnshops of Edinburgh are flooded with bogus manuscripts and spurious documents which have been sold as genuine at the quarterly auctions.

Oct. 20th, 1892. To-day I have been at work upon the Burgh Records, which I am transcribing page by page. My natural inclination has always tended towards antiquity, and I find great pleasure in revealing the past life of this old town, which lies buried in these ancient documents like some lava-strewn Roman city. I am making copious notes with a view to compiling a book, which I think might be called *Peebles in the Olden Time*. If I proceed with it, it will present a straightforward account (in modern language) of the life of the Border burghers from mediæval times onwards. For this I shall draw upon three sources: the available Records, the newspaper accounts published locally in 1870 and 1871, and the more recent *Gleanings from the Burgh Records*.

I am also translating the tale of *The Three Priests of Peebles*, which I intend to publish in modern guise, with full notes. *Peblis to the Play* is also engrossing my attention—one of my many irons in the fire! Would that I had the dynamic industry of Sir Walter Scott—to say nothing of his imaginative range! Still, archæology is my keenest pleasure, and the time is not, I think, misspent. I should like to leave some literary memorials behind me.

Dec. 17*th.* This is my thirty-second birthday. I can thank God for another year of life, of health, of work, and of domestic happiness. The birthday gifts which I most prize are a copy of the late Lord Tennyson's works from my wife, and from my mother a letter written by my father announcing my own birth, and a figured lavender vest which he wore at my christening thirty-two years ago. This I shall have made down for my own use, and shall take pleasure in wearing for association's sake.

I am at present attending a case of general paralysis of the insane. The patient can neither move, speak, hear nor see, and lies completely rigid; he can breathe, but that is all. His life is that of a vegetable rather than that of an animal. His mother, an aged frail woman, nurses him with ceaseless unwearied care, though the turning, feeding, and washing of such a case makes constant heavy work inevitable. Her endurance and devotion have taught me much.

Dec. 25*th.* We spent our Christmas Day this year in Edinburgh, and attended morning service in St Giles' Cathedral. Every seat was filled, and one gained the sense of communal worship which a crowded kirk always engenders. The sermon—a dissertation on pre-Christian mythology—did not stir me; but Handel's *Hallelujah Chorus*, which was sung as an anthem, exalted and inspired the soul. One feels instinctively that this is great music, and its triumphant strains linger long in the mind. After service, we made a tour of the Cathedral, reading history in every stone and pillar. What a pageant of Scottish story this place unfolds! The unfinished extension of the choir, dating from the days of Flodden; the Moray Aisle with its memories of the Good Regent; the grave of Montrose; the Albany expiatory chapel; and the modern Chambers Chapel, dedicated to the memory of a Peebles man —all form links in the associative chain. I never visit Edinburgh without spending an hour in St Giles', sitting for choice at the west end of the nave, a place favourable to meditation. Everything around is full of suggestion, stimulus, and historical romance. The clanging din of the city streets cannot invade the hallowed stillness. One finds here "rest after toyle, ease after warre"; contemplation spreads her wings, and one rediscovers true religion in the light of bygone centuries and changing creeds.

Dec. 31*st.* I have now kept this Journal for one year, in snatches. I sometimes ask myself "Why?" Sir Walter's example undoubtedly started me on the path; the fact that he found time, amid his voluminous writing, to achieve a similar record, encouraged me to persevere in these humble annals of a doctor's doings. A pocket-book in the local museum, compiled about the beginning of the century by a certain Dr Reid, recording his daily mileage when visiting patients, further aroused my interest. May not my own successors in this place be interested one day—say a hundred years hence—in reading of the daily professional routine of their nineteenth-century predecessor? Will they laugh over his equestrian adventures with a flesh-and-blood horse, while they are whirled from patient to patient in their electric carriages? Will they perhaps ridicule his ancient diagnoses and medical theories? Will the small Burgh of Peebles have blossomed into a thriving manufacturing city, filling the valleys and crowning the hills? Who can tell?

In any event, I propose to continue my Journal, if God will, for another year at least. I have not found it a toil, rather indeed a pleasure; and in recording those small things which go to make up life, like the threads on the weaver's loom, I have taken pains to do so in a plain, direct and absolutely accurate way. When I am dead, others may learn from these pages how a country doctor lived and worked in this remote age.

This being Hogmanay, we sat up to welcome in the New Year as usual, and my wife sang Tennyson's haunting lines for me, as is her custom every New Year's Eve:

> Ring out, wild bells, to the wild sky,
>   The flying cloud, the frosty light;
>   The year is dying in the night;
> Ring out, wild bells, and let him die.

> Ring out old shapes of foul disease;
>   Ring out the narrowing lust of gold;
>   Ring out the thousand wars of old,
> Ring in the thousand years of peace.

So ends the Old Year, and as I write the bells ring in the New.

March 1893. An inestimable benefit to our sick poor has just been inaugurated here in the establishment of a Queen's Nurse. We doctors are greatly indebted to these nurses for much valuable help and observation; and the poor have a greatly improved chance of recovery owing to their skilful, efficient, and devoted nursing. It is borne in upon me that unless one is animated by the spirit of Christ, one cannot be successful either as a doctor or as a nurse. One must have spiritual insight if one is to approach the poor, the sick, the destitute, and the fallen. Upheld by this inner vision, one can find courage, inspiration, and determination to fight disease; not otherwise.

Precautions are now being taken against the modified epidemic of smallpox which has appeared in various parts of Scotland. It has been decided by the Local Authority that we Peebles doctors shall vaccinate free of charge all persons who apply to us. This timely precaution has so far kept the burgh immune. I am kept busy, as considerable numbers have already availed themselves of the vaccination offer.

July 8th. To-day I conducted the Innerleithen Alpine Club to Dawyck Forest. These are among the most beautiful and skilfully laid-out woods in Scotland; the larches, in particular, rank with the finest and most ancient in the country. One larch-tree at Kailzie, however, is older by a single night; for the Laird of Dawyck, journeying homeward from Russia with his cherished saplings, halted there for a night. Next morning, by way of requiting the hospitality of his friend the Laird of Kailzie, Dawyck detached one sapling from his bundle and planted it on the east side of the house, where it survives to this day.

September 1893. I have just returned from a short
holiday at St Andrews, whither I went after the birth
of our second son, John Cameron, named after his
Newburgh grandfather, which took place on 16th
August.

The historic associations of the old city, which I had
never before visited, have filled my mind with a pageant
of fascinating impressions. One imbibes mediæval
ecclesiasticism in the very air, and finds history writ
large upon every stone. In front of the very house
where I lodged, Patrick Hamilton was burned in the
old persecuting days. The scene which has stamped
itself most clearly on my memory is, I think, the
prospect from St Rule's Tower. We "climbed the
steep ascent to heaven with peril, toil, and pain"; my
brother, the minister of Oxnam, was with me, and my
mother, though in her sixty-seventh year, gallantly
accompanied us. On gaining the bartizan, we found
the old grey city lying at our feet, with the Cathedral
ruins in the foreground, eloquent of the silent past
which we can still interpret, stone by stone. Lives of
old-time dwellers there rose up before us as we gazed:
burghers, soldiers, monks, philosophers, mariners; all
have played their parts in the story of St Andrews and
of Scotland. The blue sea itself, fringed with tossing
foam, forms the boundary of the city, and the green
links and yellow sand-dunes stretch away inland to the
horizon-line. One can still discern traces of three
distinct religious orders in this place. There are the
ancient Celtic crosses which form the foundations of
the Cathedral; the Church of Rome, once omnipotent,

now represented by a humble iron chapel; and, last but not least, the Church of Scotland in the person of Dr A. K. H. Boyd, who now holds unchallenged sway in the Town Kirk and in the Church of St Mary.

My brief sojourn among these stimulating scenes has refreshed me much. My mind has been re-stored with fresh images and invigorating thoughts, some of which are already emerging in versified shape.

Our infant son was the first child baptized by the new minister of Peebles, the Rev. Matthew Gardner, who has just succeeded the late Mr Lorraine in that office. He appears to be a well-read, scholarly, and intellectual man, full of nervous energy; sympathetic and kindly withal. I feel we may become friends in the future.

There has been some little difficulty over the baptism question, as the custom at present is to baptize infants in the church, at the conclusion of morning service, after the congregation have withdrawn. I am opposed to this procedure, as the point of the ceremony is, in the words of the Shorter Catechism, "the receiving of the child into the visible Church." If, then, the "visible Church," represented by the worshippers, all depart before the rite, leaving only the empty pews as witnesses, the symbolic value is lost and the ceremony deprived of half its meaning. On my propounding my views to Mr Gardner, he explained that many parents are, or profess to be, deterred from bringing their infants to church for baptism by trepidation at the thought of confronting the assembled congregation, but will readily face the ordeal if assured that the ceremony will be semi-private. In the end we arrived at a compromise: the minister announced from the pulpit that the sacrament of baptism would be administered immediately after the benediction, and that any who so desired might remain to witness it. More than half of the congregation did so, and our infant son was thus admitted to the "visible Church" in the visible presence of some of its members.

Oct. 19*th*. An odd thing happened last night. Having wandered into St Peter's (Episcopal) Church at the time of evening service, I listened with the greatest interest to an excellent sermon on the medical profession, based on the words from Ecclesiasticus: "Give place to the physician, for the Lord hath created him; let him not go from thee, for thou hast need of him. There is a time when in their hands there is good success." Naturally, I was in complete agreement with these sentiments, and considered the sermon "one of the best that ever I heard in my life," as Pepys would have said.

This morning, on meeting the parson, I complimented him warmly on his choice of subject and its treatment; and was informed that yesterday was the Festival of St Luke, the "beloved physician"; hence the apposite discourse. I could wish this festival were likewise honoured in the Kirk of Scotland, if only for its effect on non-paying and cantankerous patients!

Dec. 10*th*. I have just had a sad and tragic case of diphtheria in the windpipe of a fine, stalwart eight-year-old boy. After a consultation, as the membrane was too low down for a tube to be inserted with any benefit, we had to decide, with the parents' consent, to leave the child to die. The scene haunts me yet: we two doctors stating the stark facts, but not attempting to sway the parents either way; the agonized couple weighing their child's life in the balance, only to concur in the fateful decision. In the next room, on a couch by the fire, lay the boy—livid, perspiring, conscious, repeating my name over and over again with hoarse respiration and croaking articulation. In two beds in the same room, four younger children were merrily laughing and playing, unconscious of

Dr and Mrs Gunn

Unveiling of the Peebles war memorial, 5 October 1922. Dr Gunn is on the extreme left, next to Earl Haig. Mr Thornburn (Convenor of the county) stands centre right, with John Buchan on the extreme right.

Right.
John Buchan with Dr Gunn, 1930

Below.
Ceremony at Neidpath Castle combined with the Riding of the Marches. Cornet Veitch brings in the flag as Dr Gunn looks on

Above.
Warden of Neidpath initiation at Neidpath Castle, 1929

Left.
The Cross Kirk

Below.
Plaque commemmorating Dr Gunn at the Cross Kirk

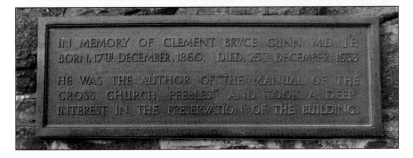

IN MEMORY OF CLEMENT BRYCE GUNN M.D. J.P.
BORN, 17TH DECEMBER, 1860. DIED, 25TH DECEMBER, 1933

HE WAS THE AUTHOR OF "THE MANUAL OF THE
CROSS CHURCH, PEEBLES" AND TOOK A DEEP
INTEREST IN THE PRESERVATION OF THE BUILDING.

Right.
Peebles Parish Church

Below.
Plaque on the pillar behind the pew where Dr Gunn sat when he attended Peebles Parish Church

HERE WAS WONT TO SIT
CLEMENT BRYCE GUNN M.D.
HISTORIAN OF
THE CHURCHES OF TWEEDDALE
AND CHRONICLER OF THE
UNRETURNING BRAVE 1914-18

'Lindores' – Dr Gunn's house in Peebles, as it is today

the grim tragedy being enacted beside them. I promptly had them removed to another room, and having left chloroform for euthanasia, if necessary, came away, leaving despair behind. Sometimes after scenes like these I am haunted by doubts of a beneficent Creator.

Jan. 30*th*, 1894. To-day I walked with the six-year-old Winifred through the snow to Neidpath Castle "to see the new baby" there. We were welcomed on the threshold by the friendliest of tame robins, which preceded us up the staircase and ushered us into the living-room. It appears that whenever a severe storm is impending, this robin, like the Roman generals invading Gaul, takes up his winter quarters in the ancient Castle and abides there until conditions become more favourable to out-of-doors activity. He is always hospitably received and plentifully fed; in short, is treated as one of the family, and does the honours of the grim old keep during his sojourn within its walls. I was reminded of the old Saxon legend which described a bird flitting from the darkness of a winter's night into the warm, firelit hall where the thanes are feasting; passing through and circling among them for a space; then taking wing once more, out into the darkness and silence of the night. The old chronicler likens the bird's transitory flight to the soul of man, which arrives from an unknown source, lingers for a brief space, and then departs, no man knows whither.

Feb. 12*th*. A patient told me to-night that when crossing Tweed Bridge lately, he came upon a man leaning over its parapet, regarding the river with concentrated gaze, and muttering abstractedly to himself the while. His curiosity aroused, my informant approached quietly, and heard these words repeated again and again in sombre, dirge-like tones: "*What a lee! Eh, what a lee! What a lee!*" Discreet inquiry elicited the facts. The man had just returned to Peebles, his native place, after many years spent in India. During the whole time of his sojourn there he had steadfastly maintained, against all comers, the statement that the River Tweed at Peebles was considerably wider than the Ganges (a mile in width!). Time had now revealed his error, and his pardonable patriotic pride reeled under the blow. I was reminded of another exile who, on revisiting these parts after a lifetime spent abroad, asked me to conduct him to the Catrail, which he had for years promised himself to visit. When I escorted him to that portion of it which is visible at Torwoodlee, his disappointment and chagrin were poignant. He had expected something similar in size and structure to the Great Wall of China! *Sic transit gloria mundi* —and particularly that glory begotten of childhood's memories, ever golden and generally deceptive.

March 13*th*, 1894. Last night the High Street of our staid old burgh was suddenly transformed into the Market Square of Hamelin. A certain Mr Christie, well known for acts of kindly benevolence, is in the habit of paying for admission for great numbers of children to every entertainment which comes to the town. A Kinderspiel was advertised to take place last night, and the street outside the hall was consequently thronged with hundreds of children, all agog with expectation and excitement. Would the magician appear? Would the portals of happiness swing back at his potent "Open Sesame"? All at once the wonder-worker came in sight, striding along the Eastgate; instantly there was a mighty rush towards him of singing, shouting children, who danced by his side and crowded after him along the street, exactly as the Hamelin bairns followed the Pied Piper of old. On reaching the hall, he paid entrance money for as many as the place would hold, and the children, still singing, surged in after him like a human tidal wave. Never have I seen a place of entertainment so packed. I had secured places for some invalid patients in the balcony; the old men from the Poor-house occupied the seats of honour. *The* spectacle of the evening was not so much the stage performance, as the unforgettable sight of those serried ranks of children, shouting and applauding in an ecstasy of delight and rapture.

March 26*th*. Much talk is being occasioned by the introduction of flowers as decoration for the church— an innovation greeted with the usual outburst of narrow-minded, conventional hostility on the part of a few. I am told that "the cloven hoof of Episcopacy" is suspected in every petal, and that "High Church tendencies" lurk under every leaf! I have expressed my view, which is that flowers, being God's own handi-work, should certainly serve to beautify and adorn the services offered to His glory. I would have them always in church, and prefer them to most man-made forms of decoration.

May 1*st*. This afternoon I made out ninety accounts: a most disagreeable and uncongenial labour. As an antidote, I then buried myself for an hour in ecclesi-astical history, seeking to sink the penniless present in the poetic past! Followed by way of refreshment, a stroll with my wife by the river through the park and towards Neidpath Castle. There we saw the Salvation Army, with its crimson banners, marching along the Castle avenue under the ancient yews, on its way to hold a meeting in the park. The Castle, solid and sardonic, seemed to comment: "One pageant more!" Its grim battlements have seen many, traversing that same avenue: royal progresses, battle arrays, hunting parties with their echoing horns, Sheriffs' Escorts; and to-day these modern banners with their defiant legend, "Go for souls, and go for the worst!" flaunt in the breeze beneath the yew-trees' shade. "Pygmies all!" the keep would seem to say.

May 10th. Old Chaucer writes that in the month of April men long to go on pilgrimage. The English April "with his showres sweete" corresponds to our Scottish May; and certainly I find myself during this month longing devoutly to make a pilgrimage to some place of rest and refreshment. Tennyson's line rings in my mind: "There is an isle of rest for thee." But it was not, I fear, written for a country doctor!

September 1st. To-day our first-born, Winifred, was launched upon the world at the age of six, setting off for the first time to pursue the path of learning. Her instructresses are to be the Misses Bewley, two delightful ladies, daughters of an Irish clergyman, who have offered to undertake the task, though they do not take pupils. We know that under their care she will have the education of the heart as well as of the head. Like the Primrose family in *The Vicar of Wakefield*, we all— father, mother, brother, and baby—assembled at the gate to speed the small scholar, and waved encouragement as she trudged away for the first time on the unknown path of knowledge, her hand clasped in that of my sister. She will have one object at least of paramount interest on which to feast her eyes in the home of her instructresses. This is none other than the christening robe for the Duke of York's infant son,[1] which the Misses Bewley, famous for the beauty of their handiwork, have been commissioned to execute. On my professional visits to their house, I have often been privileged to inspect the progress of this work of art. The frock is of the finest nainsook muslin, trimmed with Valenciennes lace; the thread used is as fine as gossamer, and as for the needles, they are like filaments of hair. The mere male, even, is struck dumb with admiration at the marvellous care and fairylike fine-

[1] The present Prince of Wales [ED.].

ness of execution which have been lavished upon this truly royal creation.

September 6th. To-day is notable as witnessing the funeral of Professor Veitch, a native of Peebles, who became Professor of Logic and Rhetoric at Glasgow University. His knowledge of Border history and poetry, though tinged with a certain didactic element, was scholarly and profound. At the funeral one saw Lord Kelvin, Lord Napier, the two Cairds, and many another distinguished Scotsman celebrated in science, literature, and philosophy.

Dec. 2nd. A missioner has arrived in the town to conduct a religious revival. I am opposed to such things on principle, having too often witnessed the evanescence of their results. Women and girls are led by these revivals to the borders of hysteria, and often beyond them, so that medical aid has to be called in to repair the ravages of emotion. The methods of irresponsible evangelists—meetings in private for anxious inquirers, afternoon prayer-meetings "for ladies only," and so forth—are often of very doubtful value. The system of confessing publicly, as most of these enthusiasts do, the sins, shortcomings, and even crimes of their past lives, leads too often to a kind of perverted glorying in wrong-doing; the recital of past evil poisons the present, instead of ennobling it. I feel, also, that while we have our own regular, trained, and competent ministers of the Gospel at work on the cure of souls, to encourage these irresponsible gospellers, with no orders or credentials, is like summoning a quack medicine-man to assist a qualified doctor in his practice, simply because these quack methods are unusual and sensational. In my experience the unhealthy excitement and emotionalism which most "revivals" engender is not only harmful, but futile; the preacher leaves the town, and with him goes the transient blaze of piety, extinguished like a spent rocket.

Dec. 6*th*. For some months past much time and thought have gone to the designing and erection of our new house on a corner site at the head of the Old Town. Plans have been drafted, modified, and re-made; we have all been assiduous in inspecting the work as it proceeds from day to day. This afternoon, with all due formality, Winifred (aged nearly seven) and George (aged four and a half) laid the keystone of the arch over the front door of our new home. I mounted the children on the scaffolding to perform the important rite; the workmen adjusted the stone, and the four small hands were duly laid upon it as it sank to its rest. Each child then spread a trowel-ful of cement over the side of the stone. Finally, with expressions of the deepest solemnity on each earnest face, they tapped the keystone thrice with a mallet, and pronounced the formula: "We declare this stone to be well and truly laid." Nothing now remained but to pay their fees as " 'prentice masons" to their fellow-workmen, which they duly did amidst general satisfaction.

Dec. 17*th*, 1894. To-day being my thirty-fourth birthday, I thank God for the blessings of good health, a sound mind, an unbroken family circle, and an increasing practice. I have written two books, and begun to build myself a house. So far, so good; but often, as I search my conscience, I am constrained to

> feel 'tis little joy
> To know I'm farther off from Heaven
> Than when I was a boy.

To-day comes news of the death in Samoa of R. L. Stevenson. Strange that he, whom we christened "The Pirate" in our old Edinburgh days, should die on a remote Pacific island, far from the scenes he knew and loved so well! Those exquisite lines of his, addressed "To S. R. Crockett," often haunt my mind as I drive along the hill-roads over the Meldons, or up the beautiful valley of Manor:

> Grey recumbent tombs of the dead in desert places,
> Standing stones on the vacant wine-red moor;
> Hills of sheep, and the howes of the silent vanished races.
> And winds austere and pure!

They might have been written of the heathery hills and bracken-covered moors which form the lonely and lovely landscapes of this part of Tweeddale—beautiful at all seasons, even in the dead hours of night. Stevenson has not had his wish after all: "Be it granted to me to behold you again in dying, Hills of home!"—unless with the inward eye he did indeed behold them at the last. Who can tell?

Dec. 24th. This has been a somewhat lurid Christmas Eve. After a quiet humdrum day, spent in visiting patients, buying Christmas gifts for the household, and attending a meeting of kirk-session anent distribution of coal to the parish poor, I was called out to a case in the evening. During my absence, a young man was brought into the surgery, shot in the right temple. It appears that he is a miner from Portobello, who is in love with a young woman here, but has suspected latterly that she is about to "give him the go-by." He persuaded her to-night to stroll with him along the Neidpath road, and there pleaded his cause once more; was repulsed, and threatened to shoot himself there and then if she still refused him. She did so, firmly and finally; whereupon the rejected one pulled a pistol from his pocket and shot himself in the darkness; bungled it, and was brought here, bleeding profusely, to await my arrival.

While alone in the surgery he disappeared, escaping into the garden, where he hid for some time, and prudently buried the pistol. We found him lurking in the summer-house, and after some trouble I got him back into the surgery and elicited the whole story.

I found a large, ugly, ragged wound in the temple down to the bone; dressed it, and smuggled him out by the back door to lodgings where he could spend the rest of the night.

My wife and the servants were considerably alarmed by these happenings; the children, fortunately, were all in bed, and I suppose set down any disturbance they heard to the nocturnal activities of Santa Claus! So ends a love drama which must have been a tragedy had the hero been a better marksman than Providence saw fit to make him!

Dec. 29*th*. Press notices of my two books recently published (*Lays of St Andrews* and *The Three Priests of Peebles*) are now appearing. For the most part these are pleasant and encouraging. Yet I wonder sometimes whether there is any true poetry in these writings of mine. Sonnet-making is a real pleasure and passion to me, and forms my one relaxation in a busy life; but time is lacking to polish and perfect these random verses. Strange that nearly all the critics unite in praising two stanzas from the poem "On the Tower" as being the finest in the book! The lines are these:

> O 'tis hard to die in summer,
> When the fields are all aglow
> With living sheen and lovely green
> That naught of fading know.
>
> But winds must howl and dead leaves fall
>   And beauty lifeless lie,
> Ere hope grows cold and life grows old,
>   And I lie down to die!

These "Lays" have been composed at odd times and in odd places: on the moor-roads, driving in the trap, and in solitary hill-cottages all over the countryside. During long country journeys I have beguiled the weary hours by turning and reshaping a line here, a line there; by striving for a smoother rhythm or more expressive phrase. Many of these sonnets, rough-cast in my mind, have been wrought to completion on night journeys under the silent stars.

Similarly with the *Three Priests*, that ancient classic which I have taken so much pleasure in clothing in modern garb; when summoned by night to attend some shepherd's wife away in a distant valley, I took with me two companions: the old vernacular copy of *The Priests*, borrowed from the Advocates' Library, and Jameson's *Scottish Dictionary*. Then, between times, I could translate a line or two from the old-world language and turn them into modern Scots; the periods of enforced inaction passed quickly, and on the way home I would rearrange the material in my mind, or hammer out a clearer definition of some obscure phrase. All this has been healthful mental exercise if nothing more; has recreated the mind jaded by professional anxieties; has changed the current of thought, helped me to forget many cares, and sent me back to daily work with a fresher brain and clearer vision.

Hogmanay, 1894. At four in the morning I was called up to attend a maternity case, which I am well aware will develop into a bad debt, though the patient's husband is in work, and could pay if willing. My bad debts during the past year or two have amounted to 40 per cent. Nevertheless, some time ago I resolved that I would attend all poor patients who applied, and refuse none. My reason is this: I earnestly endeavour, so far as I can, to approach the suffering poor in the spirit of Christ. I have no money to give them; nor am I fitted to offer them the consolation of good words spoken in season. But this one thing I can and will do: attend the poor without payment; and that must be my religious duty henceforward. On this the last night of the year, I reaffirm the above decision in a spirit of earnest resolve.

Feb. 26*th*, 1895. For nine weeks we have been visited by the heaviest snowstorms and severest frost I can remember during my whole career. Beginning in the last week of the old year, these conditions have continued without intermission; all field work has been at a standstill, and sheep have had to be fed with carted hay and turnips. Labourers, more especially masons, have been suffering severely from unemployment and want; even the joys of unlimited curling, day after day, have begun to pall on the farmers and workmen, who are now all praying for a thaw. Plumbers keep up their spirits by anticipation of the merry time in prospect, when the great harvest of burst pipes, after the prolonged frost, will bring much grist to their mill. No work has been possible on our new house for many weeks; we are all suffering from hope deferred, but the children console themselves by learning to skate on Tweed, which is entirely frozen over. It is amusing to watch their daily progress on the icebound river, safeguarded from accident by wearing stout rope cables, which our Irish coachman controls from the bank with admirable patience and discretion.

The general health of the community under these severe and prolonged conditions has not suffered acutely; but the weak and chronically ill have, in many cases, gone under, and those at the two extremes of life have succumbed in large numbers.

August 31*st*, 1895. Yesterday was our last day in this house, the first home of our married life and the birthplace of three children. To-day we moved into our new abode—as yet nameless, but probably to be christened Lindores, after the famous Fifeshire Abbey round which cluster so many personal memories. Some regrets are inevitable on leaving the home of eight happy years; we have known much joy within these walls, and no sorrow. That is to come.

The new house is of course as yet in confusion;

furniture stacked in hall and passages, floors still wet with fresh varnish, draughts abounding everywhere: the usual accompanients of a newly built dwelling. In every moment I can spare from being a doctor, I become a "flitter," moving bookcases and so forth with the invaluable help of the coachman, who has been a literal tower of strength during the removal operations. He contrives to add to goodwill, patience: to patience, resource; and to all, unwearied and un-failing humour, which counts for much.

To-night—our first in the new home which I have built—though too weary to "overflow in a sonnet," as my brother terms this failing, I jot down the following lines, to be completed at leisure:

> Above an ebb and flow this roof will poise
> And underneath, while glows the hearth, a tide
> Will flow of living, loving girls and boys . . .
> But likewise, ebbing life will mar the joys,
> And one day smoke will rise, and windows in the morn
> Grow bright, though pass the Founder to the tryst
> Which all must keep:—God grant his soul meet Christ!

Sept. 6th. To-day the shaft of the ancient Cross of Peebles, dating probably from about 1320, was success-fully removed, unbroken, from the unsuitable site to which it has for some time been relegated, and set up anew on a pedestal, provided by William Thorburn as a gift to the Burgh, at the east end of the main street. In olden days, many a delinquent has been bound to this ancient pillar, with a parchment on his breast recounting his misdeeds. All public proclamations were wont to be made from its base, and the health of successive sovereigns drunk round its pediment for many generations. Now that this historic shaft is once more mounted aloft in an outstanding position, it will serve as the palladium of the rights and privileges of this ancient Royal Burgh.

Sept. 21st. This afternoon my wife and I, with some

friends, visited Traquair House—the oldest inhabited house in Scotland—and were shown over its historic treasures by the four brothers Maxwell-Stuart, the present owners. All evening this ancient dwelling has haunted my imagination. History breathes through every nook and cranny of the place. In the library are many beautifully illuminated missals and prayer-books, of exquisite workmanship. Some of these, the work of monkish hands long dead, probably occupied several successive lives ere they were completed. On the green lawn and courtyard of the house, what scenes have been enacted throughout the centuries! Hunting meets, hangings, funeral pageants, Court assemblies: all have come and passed. To-day the same trees looked on, as they have done from generation to generation; and the shadows followed the sunbeams over the grass, as the shades will succeed the sunshine of our own lives when we too pass into eternal silence.

Oct. 2nd. My patient, Dr Turnbull Smith, told me to-day, apropos his recent purchase of the *Encyclopædia Britannica*, a curious anecdote. He and a friend, while on a fishing holiday in the Highlands, went one Sunday to attend service at the Parish Church of Carnock. The church appeared to be completely deserted: no worshippers, no elders, no beadle. So one of the two visitors rang the bell, and the other ushered the minister up the pulpit steps. An orderly service followed, and an excellent and outstanding sermon, of which they had the sole benefit. Thereafter the two friends adjourned with the minister to the manse; and he informed them that his ostra-cized position was due to the vehement Free Kirk partisanship which infested the whole district. All his so-called parishioners were members of that body, and regarded himself and his pulpit as anathema. "Many of them," he concluded, "will go a mile out of their way rather than pass my manse." "Then how, in heaven's name," inquired the visitors, "do you keep your mind alert and your soul alive?" The ostracized minister pointed to the massive volumes of the *Encyclopædia Britannica* which adorned his study shelves: "By reading *that* from A to Z; I've been through it once already, and am now at B for the second time." This indomitable fortitude had a pleasing sequel. Time passed; autumn came, and with it a shooting-party to the mansion-house. In those orthodox days, the lady of the manor, with her guests, went to church every Sunday when in residence as a matter of course. She was so deeply impressed by the minister's abilities and eloquence that she seized the opportunity, when it arose, to present the Encyclopædic scholar to the living and parish of Paisley Abbey! From thence to St Giles' Cathedral, Edinburgh, was but a step; and thus the Reverend James Lees, the unknown minister of a remote Highland parish with no congregation, blossomed into the Very Reverend Dr Cameron Lees, one of the Queen's Chaplains: and all owing to the *Encyclopædia Britannica*!

Nov. 3rd. Five days ago (Oct. 29th) the Parish Church of Peebles completed its seven hundredth year of continuous religious life. On 29th October A.D. 1195, the Church of St Andrew, whose tower still stands in the churchyard, was dedicated to the worship of God. It has known many vicissitudes since those far-off days; existed for over two centuries as the Cross Kirk, whose ruins still stand, though in a deplorably neglected condition; reverted to its old patron, St Andrew, from 1784-1885; and for the past eight years has been housed in the new building, which from its commanding position dominates the town like a cathedral.

For some time I have been conferring with the minister (Mr Gardner, now my principal friend and companion in Peebles) anent this anniversary. At his request I have supplied him with notes and chronological data of the church's history during the seven centuries of its existence. This morning he preached from the text, "Remember the days of old, consider the years of many generations," an eloquent and forcible discourse, into which he had skilfully welded the historical data I had furnished, adorning it with much apt and arresting material of his own.

I have also caused to be inserted in the wall of the new song-school a tablet commemorating the fact that this school was re-established in the seven hundredth year of the church; so that the song-men and singing-boys of unborn generations may not forget their heritage.

Nov. 18*th.* All yesterday I was tired and over-wrought, suffering from nervous exhaustion due to pressure of work. "Physician, heal thyself," is no text for a country doctor; he has no time to fulfil it. To make matters worse, at 2 A.M. I was urgently summoned to attend a woman with whom fried eggs had disagreed! Later a maternity case haled me forth again at 4.30 A.M. To-day, however, a patient has cheered me with an anecdote *à propos* of the decay of religious life in Scotland. Some years ago, when travelling in England, he overheard one commercial traveller complaining to another that no business could be done in Glasgow owing to the inveterate churchgoing habits of its citizens. "I arrived late on a Wednesday night, and told the waiter at my hotel that I should make an early start with business calls next day. 'No use; it's the Fast Day,' said he; 'they'll all be at the kirk.' I therefore spent the day, with other guests from the hotel, at a place called 'Doon-the-watter,' where we enjoyed ourselves and drank a fair amount. Friday I had to spend in bed with a headache; Saturday, the waiter told me, was again barred; 'they'll all be at the kirk.' And so they were! Sunday of course was 'the Sabbath'; but would you believe it, they were all at the kirk on the Monday again! In despair I questioned the hotel proprietor as to what sect of Christians these extraordinary people could be; he replied: 'They're no' Christians; they're maistly Free Kirk!' So away I came, no forrader than when I went. Never again!"

My patient supplied the unlucky Englishman with the "reasons annexed" to his misfortunes: he had arrived during the half-yearly Communion season, when in those stricter days "the preachings" occupied, in addition to the "Lord's Day" itself, the Thursday (Fast Day), the Saturday (preparatory services), and the Monday (thanksgiving services). Times are not what they were!

April 25th, 1896. To-night I returned to duty after a week's holiday at Stichill Manse, where my wife and the children are remaining for a time as the guests of my brother George. It has been a golden week of perfect peace, tonic and recreating. We enjoyed the tranquillity of a country Sabbath; the children helped to ring the church bell for the three services, to their great satisfaction and the diversion of the beadle. We visited the village school, where the scholars sang to us very sweetly, and we then provided a "scatter" of 5 lb. of sweets as a recompense. In that quiet country manse one finds a peace obtainable nowhere else. My locum tenens here considers himself half-killed with work; yet his visits have been less by one hundred than my average for the week!

May 27th. I began the day by giving chloroform to a patient undergoing teeth extraction by the dentist. Dental decay is extremely widespread and rapid here in Peebles, and extractions are frequent. I attribute this to soft drinking water, low temperature, and too much over-cooked and softened food.

Later, I came upon a derelict child of four, lost by

her vagrant parents, and spent some time seeking and finding lodgings for her. The wee girl was wandering about in the greatest distress, feeling herself abandoned in a friendless world; but cheered up later when I left her in kindly hands. I was reminded of a poem by Blake, *The Little Girl lost*.

To-night, driving home very late from a country visit, we passed several carts loaded with families, their *lares et penates*, "flitting" from one outlying farm to another. Among the furniture and bundles which crowded the farm-wagons, children of all ages were huddled together, sleeping or waking by turns; the infants, wrapped in shawls, lay cradled in their mothers' arms. The night was warm and soft, and the summer wind kindly. It was a scene to which Hardy the novelist could have done ample justice.

June 8th. Last night, as I went down the Old Town to pay a visit, an open trap passed me, driving towards Neidpath Castle. In it was seated a minister, the Rev. David Mitchell, on his way home to the manse of Kirkurd; he greeted me pleasantly, and passed on. To-night at the same hour, on the same spot, I was met by a hearse containing his dead body, on its way home to the manse of Kirkurd! His greeting to me yesterday was, though neither of us knew it, *Moriturus te saluto*; mine to-night was a salutation to the dead. On his homeward way last night from Peebles, where he had been preaching, his horse shied; he turned faint and ill, was driven back to the town, and died almost immediately. The text from which he preached yesterday was: "There stood by me this night the Angel of God, whose I am and whom I serve."

· *Sept. 27th.* To-day, Peebles Parish Church blazes like a star in the firmament of ecclesiastical liberality. The sum of no less than £1365 has been obtained from the offertories of this single Sunday, for the joint purposes of erecting a Church Hall and avoiding a

Bazaar! Last Sunday the minister announced that in order to obviate the endless worries and vexations inseparable from that holy terror, a Church Bazaar, he would appeal to the congregation to-day to enclose in sealed envelopes their promises of support, which he hoped would amount to £1000. Sceptics abounded; cold water was liberally thrown; it was feared that the dreaded Bazaar was, after all, a predestined calamity. But this phenomenal offertory has saved the situation, silenced the scoffers, and astonished all concerned.

To-day has been a memorable one for me also, as I have ushered no fewer than four infants into this weary world. I was called out of church midway in the sermon for No. One; drove several miles into the country, and on the homeward journey was summoned some distance out of my way to No. Two. I did not reach home till six in the evening, having had neither bite nor sup since breakfast. A third summons at eight o'clock eventuated in twins at eleven P.M.! It is now midnight; babies Nos. Three and Four are safely launched upon their earthly pilgrimage. "And so to bed."

New Year's Day, 1897. Immediately after the midnight service in church, when the New Year was but a few minutes old, the minister and I set off together to "first-foot" a dying man. We found him wrestling with death in the form of pleuro-pneumonia. The minister prayed by his bed; I administered oxygen. It was a strange ironic beginning to the New Year, and brought us up short, as it were, on the threshold of eternity.

This evening our children entertained eight of the raggedest urchins we could discover, to a feast of fun, games, and abundant eatables; all were happy, and the three small hosts amused their guests with the utmost tact, resource, and goodwill.

Attention has lately been attracted in the literary world to the abilities of a young nephew of my friend William Buchan, Town Clerk of Peebles. This new writer, John Buchan,[1] though not yet twenty-one years of age, has already published more than one work of fiction. His local colour is skilfully drawn from the glens and hopes and valleys of Peeblesshire and Lanarkshire. *John Burnett of Barns* holds perhaps the keenest interest for the folk of Tweeddale. It is, I think, more than probable that a great future lies in store for this gifted "lad o' pairts."

Feb. 8th. To-day a poor woman aged thirty-eight, the mother of ten children, whom I have been attending twice daily without fee since last June, has died of cancer, after untold suffering. When I first began to attend her, she was living at an outlying farm, where her husband worked. I persuaded his master to release him—no easy task, he being a good and valuable workman as well as a kind, attentive husband—and found him a situation here in the town at a weekly wage of £1. I also secured places for two of the children in the mills; and finally, after much difficulty, found a house vacant, in which the whole family could be lodged at a rent of two shillings weekly. Having thus arranged matters for the household, I had the mother removed one fine summer evening on a litter, from the farm to the town. Since then I have been able to visit her twice daily (in all, I have seen her over five hundred times), and the Queen's Nurse has also attended her frequently. I have just made out my daily list of patients for to-morrow, and for the first time for nine months her name will not head the page. Yet it is something to have been able to ease the slow progression of such anguish towards its inevitable (and welcome) consummation.

June 21st. The spirit of Jubilee has descended upon Peebles. Nothing is talked of but the celebrations of Her Majesty's great day to-morrow. Business is at a standstill, flags and flowers pervade the town, and

[1] Now Lord Tweedsmuir, Governor-General of Canada [ED.].

to-night all the citizens are abroad to inspect their triumphal arches *et hoc genus omne*. Various plans for this Diamond Jubilee celebration have been mooted during the past months, the most picturesque being the lighting of a chain of beacons from the old peel towers of the Border. My own cherished project was that of the opening-up and beautifying of the ruined Cross Kirk, and the conversion into a green pleasance of the present howling wilderness around it. But this is a dream which must, I fear, wait years yet for fulfilment, if indeed fulfilment ever comes! I will not, however, abandon hope of its eventual realization. Meanwhile, in preparation for the Riding the Marches to-morrow, I got into the saddle this afternoon, for the first time for ten years, and rode to Lyne Toll and back by way of rehearsal!

Jubilee Day (*June 22nd*). In common with the rest of Her Majesty's subjects, we have spent an arduous and enthusiastically loyal day. We rode the Marches—a distance of about six miles—in the morning, when Peter (my horse) acquitted himself with all decorum under novel conditions. I hurried off afterwards to pay professional visits, and finished my round just in time to join the assemblage round the newly installed Cross in the High Street, to sing the National Anthem and listen to the loyal address. Public sports, games for the children, fireworks, and bonfires consumed the rest of the day; the accidental conflagration at one fell swoop of the whole remaining stock of fireworks provided the most sensational display of the evening, but otherwise all went well. We heard with pleasure to-night that Her Majesty, in London, has safely survived the fatigues of the day, with no untoward accident. We have now (midnight) removed our flags and loyal decorations from the house; and so ends the Diamond Jubilee, a milestone in our day and generation.

August 31st. To-day I attended a solemn and

sorrowful pageant at Dawyck, when the young heir, Ernest Roxburgh Balfour, a stalwart athlete of twenty-three, was brought home dead, to take possession of his new heritage in his coffin. He had been staying in the Perthshire Highlands, and died there after a short illness. His body was carried on a farm-cart, the coffin draped with the flag of his University barge. From Dawyck grounds to the old churchyard it was borne shoulder-high through the green forest glades, his fellow-oarsmen taking the first and last relays. The slow procession, wending its way under the ancient trees, was both striking and sorrowful; one pictured the joyous home-coming which should have welcomed him to lands and gear; the speech-making, the banqueting, the bonfires blazing far into the night. Now, instead of the handful of earth with which an heir is wont to claim his new heritage, he takes sasine with six feet of kirkyard sod. When the coffin had been lowered, we entered the ancient Parish Church, and there listened to an eloquent and arresting oration by the Rev. Cosmo Gordon Lang, Vicar of Portsea, one of the Queen's favourite chaplains. This able clergyman of the Church of England, whose father was Moderator of the Scottish Chuich, impressed me greatly by his moving eloquence; he will assuredly become a bishop one day.[1] We had left the open grave amid a storm of rain, under lowering skies; but as we emerged from the church the sun shone out serene and golden, and what had been a yawning gap in the green turf was now a rainbow carpet of flowers. Thus the Heir of Dawyck came home. Some lines of Matthew Arnold's have echoed in my mind all day, anent the

> cabined, ample spirit
> It fluttered and failed for breath;
> To-night it doth inherit
> The vasty hall of Death.

---

[1] The present Archbishop of Canterbury [ED.].

CHAPTER VIII

LONDON IN THE 'NINETIES—THE
MACHINE AGE DAWNS—ADVEN-
TURES BY AUTOMOBILE

May 28*th*, 1898. Mr Gladstone was buried to-day.
In the evening we attended a public demonstration
of the phonograph—a new invention which has just
penetrated to Peebles. We heard two eloquent
speeches from Mr Gladstone, whose funeral took
place a few hours earlier, delivered with marvellous
energy and transmitted with the utmost distinctness,
every word clear and incisive. Science has fulfilled
the text, "He being dead yet speaketh."

June 22*nd*. Our fourth child, Irene, was born to-day
at Lindores. All is well with mother and child; I
have much to thank God for. The Beltane Festival is
being held as usual this week in the town; to which
we shall add a nativity festival of our own.

October 15*th*. A message came in late at night from
Lour, above Stobo, summoning me thither at once.
So away we drove amid torrents of rain, through inky
darkness, with a fierce wind howling. The lamps
of the trap would not stay lit, owing to the violence
of the gale; our hats we first held on, then placed
below the seat; the rugs were tossed about, and
nothing could keep the rain out.

At last, about midnight, we reached the railway
station at Stobo, where I expected someone to be
waiting to guide me. Not a soul appeared. We
knocked up the blacksmith, and asked him to put up
man and horse in his smithy; he agreed. The forge
furnace was stirred into a blaze, the doors closed;
horse, trap, and man housed; and all wet wraps
hung up to dry. Carrying my bag and one carriage-
lamp, I then began my tramp to Lour. First I crossed
the railway; then waded the flooded haughs, up to

the knees, the rising torrent raging alongside; stumbling against hillocks, floundering in hollows, and coming perilously near the enormously swollen river. Peering through the ghostly mirk, I at last spied the crazy suspension-bridge, swaying over the bed of Tweed. With considerable danger I reached and crossed its rickety length. More flooded haughs to be forded knee-deep; then at length, firmer ground as far as Dawyck Mill. Now for the ascent of the hill. No light streams down from the cottage; blackness all round; lamp blown out; cloak but a burden hampering and tripping me; my bag seems heavier each minute. Up and up, till at length I fear the path is lost; I grow breathless and spent. Suddenly a faint beam of light; up once more; and a last spurt towards the lighted house.

I scolded the man for his delay, but his defence was good. He had been away all day with a shooting-party; his wife in labour from midday; he had come in at eight, rushed down ere the storm broke, wired for me, and rushed home again to assist his wife. She had been quite alone all day! I was in time, attended her, left her with her baby, and got down, along the haughs, across Tweed, and home without accident— thank God.

November 13th. To-day I have been struck by a feeling akin to reverence which a doctor experiences when meeting those persons whom he knows to be carrying about with them a mortal disease. Sometimes the patient knows it, and like the Spartan youth carries the gnawing agony concealed from public gaze, but ever reminding him of its dread presence. Such is a case of cirrhotic Bright's Disease in a woman whom I met this morning. She was staggering in vertigo over Tweed Bridge; her sight has grown so dim that she did not know me, her doctor. Her husband died from the same disease, hence her knowledge of the symptoms, of their steady advance, and of the uselessness of all medical aid. Withal, she is brave and composed—a woman to respect for her calmness, fortitude, and resignation.

Opposite her lives the mother of a large family, who has an inoperable cancer, and does not know it. There is no pain, but weakness and hæmorrhage. She is a patient who must not know. I have to assume an impassive, non-committal mask when confronting her questioning gaze. She can still cope with her domestic tasks, with an occasional day in bed. But the relentless enemy is there, ever stealing an insidious advance upon the unsuspecting victim.

Then the consumptives! One meets them daily, though they are fewer in this district owing to the absence of clay. The cold here is not a damp-ground coldness, but a sharp, dry product of the east wind or of frost; and the east wind is well dried from the salt rawness of the ocean by its passage over the southlands of the Borders. Most consumptives are hopeful to the last. One such died in my practice this morning, after lingering on in a living death for a month. Only yesterday I sent to the asylum a young married man with that most awful of all diseases, general paralysis of the insane. Daily has he walked the country roads, with his ataxic gait and expressionless features. A fatuous good-humour deceived his own mother, who never realized that anything serious could ail her son who took his meals so well. What a brave devoted wife he has! A young girl with a little daughter— her second baby died—she has now to return to the mill and work to keep the little home together. But the strain, with the anxiety, was wearing her out; now she will have the work alone. Her life of un-selfish devotion to her stricken man is one of the sermons preached to us doctors, and to the neighbours, day by day.

To meet these patients on the street, to chat with them about the weather, to remark upon some parochial gossip in an unconcerned way—such are among the deadly ironies in a general practitioner's life. "Those about to die salute thee" is the daily greeting of these condemned ones—*les avertis*—of whom never a day passes but one sees at least one. "Madam, have you any commands for the next world?" was the dying remark of Robert Burns to Mrs Riddell. One sometimes feels as though these doomed yet cheerful persons might well ask the baffled doctor the same question. And yet, sometimes the doctor himself meets death first. I recall one who, when lecturing on Locomotor Ataxia, wished to demonstrate to his class the patellar tendon reflex; he struck his own limb below the knee, and lo, it did not respond! That man went home, set his house in order, and died. For him the writing was already on the wall.

November 29th. To-day the Sirdar, Lord Kitchener, received the Freedom of the City of Edinburgh. He is one of the most wonderful men of this century. One has greatly admired his minute attention to the smallest details of the late Soudan campaign; the caim determination which made him hold back his advance till every preparation had been completed for the next move; his total absence of self-advertisement; his restraint in refraining from all excesses which often follow victory; and, moreover, the man's complete belief in himself. Were I not a husband and father, I should like to go to Khartoum, and have some share in that great Gordon Memorial College for which the Sirdar is now asking £100,000. Gordon has not died in vain; he would cheerfully have given his life to know that the result of his sacrifice would be the establishment of this vast civilizing agency in the heart of the Soudan. These are the men who convince one that it is worth while to have lived. Each year, on the anniversary of Gordon's death, my children place a spray of evergreens beneath the bronze bust of him which they gave me on a recent birthday, and we salute his memory in silent reverence.

January 1st, 1899. To-day sees the outbreak of that perennial question—"When does the new century begin?" Some think it is at the end of this year of 1899; others, at the beginning of 1901. The Kaiser, Lord Kelvin, and our Peebles minister, Mr Gardner, all maintain the first hypothesis; but the Pope, Professor Tait, and many others, give pride of place to 1st January 1901. Discussion rages both verbally and in the newspapers, and frequently from pulpits; but in the main, evidence as well as predilection lippens to the conviction that the new century will begin on 1st January 1901.

I brought in the New Year to-day in the black-smith's house at Hall-Lyne. I drove thither at eleven o'clock on New Year's Eve, and returned home at 3 A.M. At 5 A.M. I was recalled, brought home the baby, and came back once more at 9 A.M. This is the best of all methods of bringing in the New Year— at work. *Laborare est orare.*

January 23rd. To-day I saw in a house a woman patient reading *The Flying Roll*. This production of a religious fanatic, or at least of one who had an overweening belief in his own powers, has had some vogue recently here and in Edinburgh. The writer's professional name is James Jezreel. He deals with the affairs of Anglo-Israel, though whether he means that the British are the ten lost tribes, or that they inherit the privileges of the aforesaid ten tribes, is not apparent. The headquarters of this sect were at New Brompton, near Chatham, where the remains of a vast uncompleted building, like a Norman keep, attest alike their ambitious designs for a temple and their failure to accomplish their aims. James J. Jezreel was the founder both of the belief and of the temple. *The Flying Roll* was the revelation which he announced he had received direct from heaven. The building stood, or stands, four-square, and is battlemented. When Jezreel died, the cause was taken up by his wife. On her death, a few years later, the mission lost vitality and gradually dwindled, till now there are but few believers left, and the temple still stands unfinished. A strange monument to a strange fanaticism!

March 3rd, 1899. To-day's principal event did not occur till night; and a very sad matter it was. A bonny bright twelve-year-old girl, with a wealth of long thick brown hair, put in the day as usual in splendid health and good spirits. She attended school, where she was brightest in class, and in the evening, having learned her lessons, went out to meet her destiny!

She entered the premises of a local laundry and began skipping on the concrete floor, with the rope twined around her wrists. Suddenly the loop of rope caught upon the upright revolving shaft in the middle of a large iron drying-tub, and drew her into its centre. The apparatus was used for drying clothes by centrifugal action; the upright shaft revolved 500 times per minute. The whole accident occurred in a twinkling, before the machine could be stopped. The poor child was irresistibly drawn in; her long, beautiful hair proved her ruin; it wound round the shaft, and caused the entire scalp to be drawn off the head. Her left hand was severed at the wrist-joint, all but the thumb; and the left upper arm smashed in two places.

She was conveyed on an ironing-board to her parents' house, which she had left so brightly but a few minutes before.

There I found her lying on the floor. I sent for the scalp, which was brought from the laundry in four pieces. These I denuded of hair, and sewed in place again, replacing the ears as well as possible. I then severed the skin which held the hand to the wrist, and set the left humerus. At this moment her own doctor arrived and I left, after giving him final assistance, and administering a hypodermic injection of morphia. It will be almost a mercy if she die.

Query. Why in the providence of God is such pain and agony allowed? What can be its purpose?

Note (some months later).—Contrary to all expectation, this child made a fine recovery, and now goes about wonderfully well, with a good scalp, and no contraction of the features. Her exceptionally brave disposition and sunny nature have materially helped her in throwing off the after-effects of shock.

March 28*th*. I called to-day at the Peeblesshire Poorhouse, and there examined an old vagrant woman, aged eighty-three, with a view to ascertaining whether or not she is a certifiable lunatic. She is a destitute tramp, in her dotage, accustomed all her life to a vagrant career, and impatient of restraint, confinement, and discipline. She indulges in occasional outbursts of rage, often accompanied by oaths and threats of violence.

I was shown some garments, very much the worse for wear, which she had torn to tatters one day in a fit of impatience.

I have known her for many years, and have often had long talks with her. To-day she knew me perfectly well; she also knew where she was, and why. She admitted that occasionally she was subject to a "*rapture*," as she styled her outbursts; but she knows perfectly what she is doing, and can answer questions lucidly and rationally.

Having tramped the roads in all weathers, winter and summer, for over sixty years, she naturally hates the restrictions of the Poorhouse, where I have sent her repeatedly, and is always on the look-out for a means of escape, so that she may resume her normal vagrant life. However, we parted friends; I cautioned her against too many "*raptures*" in the future, but declined to certify her, as she is by no means insane, merely more logical in her desires than most of us!

August 7th. For some time past I have not been feeling very strong; find myself easily tired, and the nervous system depressed. I have therefore had to suspend all literary work, doing only my legitimate professional business. This has been a severe discipline and disappointment to me, but some rest is essential if I am to recover my nervous energy. One must simply "stick in" and work as far as possible, and not weakly succumb. What an irony of fate if just now, when outward affairs are going well with me, I were laid aside incurably, as my father was so early! However, "he that tholes, overcomes."

To-day a patient sent me R. L. Stevenson's *Underwoods* as a present. I have been re-reading "The Counterblast," which is full of sound Stoic philosophy:

> My bonny man, the warld, it's true,
> Was made for neither me nor you;
> It's just a place to warstle through,
>   As Job confessed o't;
> And aye the best that we can do
>   Is mak' the best o't . . .
> To a steigh brae, a stubborn back
>   Addressin' daily;
> An' up the rude, unbieldy track
>   O' life, gang gaily.

September 15th. Everyone is horrified and enraged at the verdict of "Guilty" in the Dreyfus case, which has recently been causing such a sensation in France, and also in our own country. History repeats itself: to-day, the innocent Jew Dreyfus is condemned, if not to death, to degradation and possibly to torture; two thousand years ago, the innocent Jew Jesus met the same verdict. And so, no doubt, it will be again and yet again.

Rumours of a possible outbreak of war with the Transvaal are everywhere current; things look very black there, and people here talk of little else.

October 9th. To-morrow I set off on an adventure which, if not precisely the rest-cure I had prescribed (in vain) for myself some weeks ago, will at any rate provide a complete change of scene, and should prove tonic.

A wealthy patient whom I have been attending at the Hydropathic here required medical escort on the journey back to his London home, and has invited me to accompany him, and to remain for a fortnight as his guest.

October 10th (London). We left Peebles in the throes of its annual Fair Day this morning, on our way to the metropolis, thus reversing the attitude of the Ettrick Shepherd, who put the claims of St Boswell's Fair before those of a Royal Coronation! On arrival we drove with the sick man in an ambulance carriage for six and a half miles, through streets crowded with horse traffic, cyclists and pedestrians, to Streatham Hill, where my patient's home is. The scene—it was between eight and nine in the evening—was a nocturne in gold and black. I greatly admired the coachman's skill in negotiating the thronged thoroughfares—no easy matter, in such a labyrinthine maze.

October 11th. This house is situated in a retired suburb, very quiet and rural; indeed it has gates at both ends, and neither heavy traffic nor funeral processions are allowed to pass. My host, a wholesale silk merchant, has a large warehouse in St Paul's Churchyard, with a staff of sixty, all most impressive in tile hats and frock coats.

To-day, in Westminster Abbey, among all the tombs of princes and statesmen, poets and queens, I was more moved by one small effigy than by all the rest: a wee baby in a marble cradle, under a marble quilt edged with fine filigree lace, holding her nursery in the hall of kings, and receiving the pitying homage of three centuries.

3.10 P.M. At this moment, in a crowded day, we witnessed what may prove to be a turning-point in Britain's national history. War with South Africa has definitely broken out, on the expiration of the Transvaal's forty-eight-hours Ultimatum; and this afternoon as we stood outside the Stock Exchange we heard the strains of *God save the King* sung by the members within, to mark the official Declaration of War. It echoed with a strange momentous sound there in the heart of the Empire, with London's millions surging at the gates; and one could not but recall Antony's sinister phrase from *Julius Cæsar*: "Cry havoc, and let slip the dogs of war!"

In the evening, to Drury Lane, in excellent company (as Pepys would say), and there witnessed a long and gorgeously spectacular drama entitled *Hearts are Trumps*. I was more interested in the historic building, with its thousand traditions of the English stage, than in the piece itself; but Vice was duly punished (by an avalanche descending from Alpine peaks) and Virtue triumphed, to live happy ever after. Thus all were satisfied; drove home, and so to bed.

Oct. 15*th* (London). To-night, on the eve of my return to Peebles, where "the trivial round, the common task" await me once more, I summarize my impressions of this London visit. It has been pleasant, restorative, and reanimating to body and mind alike; will supply energy for the coming winter, with its inevitable stress and strain; and remain a cheering memory for months to come.

While here, I have been exhaustively studied by the Cockneys as a specimen of the Scottish doctor fresh from his native wilds; have returned with interest the inquisitive stares which such novelties evoke; and have done what I can to uphold the honour of Scotland, while in my keeping!

During the visit we have replenished the inner man at the Trocadero, famous for grilled steaks; at Pagani's, whose *forte* is cutlets, and at Frascati's, where there is the best orchestra in London; champagne each night at dinner has added to our joy!

Driving about the streets with my hosts in an open landau, barouche, or hansom, I have been greatly struck by the marvellous and despotic power wielded so quietly by the police in traffic control. At a single gesture from one of these Olympians, the advancing waves of traffic recede, like the Red Sea, to allow perhaps one solitary pedestrian to cross in safety, with the peculiar leisurely gait adopted by all Londoners on such occasions. Obedient to police authority, the cabbies develop uncanny skill and daring in their difficult task; wheels graze wheels; one expects to see the scattered brains of cyclists strewing the roadway; yet a collision is rare.

I find the private houses, viewed from without, most disappointing, the very best not approaching our Edinburgh houses. Marlborough House, Devonshire House, the dwellings in Park Lane, Harley Street, Grosvenor Street, etc., have all disappointed me as to exterior effect. Too much naked red brick, and architecture resembling that of a stable. The Albert Memorial repays study; not so its neighbour the Albert Hall. The parks and open spaces, most of them adorned with lakes, are places of beauty, and must bring refreshment to those who cannot compass Nature's healing by other means.

But the great thrill, after all, is to mount on the top of a bus, and from that vantage-point view the changing panorama of the London streets at any hour of day or night. All is haste and bustle; no one wastes a

moment; frock-coated, tile-hatted men, hurrying along
Cheapside, snatch an apple from a coster's basket and
munch it as they hasten along. The stream of humanity rushes past, each unit intent on his own progress.
One knows then the sensations of the small fly on the
gigantic wheel; and that sense of utter loneliness only
possible in a vast crowd.

Hallowe'en (Peebles). Our coachman had, as usual,
prepared four turnip-lanterns for the children's
Hallowe'en celebration; but to-night, ere they could
be lit, comes terrible news of a British reverse in Natal,
and this takes the heart out of all festivity. However,
we lit our lanterns; hope must not be quenched. This
war in the Transvaal fills one with sorrow and acute
apprehension; the end no man can foresee. We
doctors, throughout the country, are attending the
families of all men serving at the front, without fee.

Nov. 23rd. For some time I have held a weekly
ambulance class for stretcher-bearers in my surgery,
after my usual evening consulting hour; a useful
though humble form of war-work which I must make
time to carry through.

To-night an amusing incident occurred: the class
were all assembled, each supplied with an arm-bone
for purposes of study, and with a living model for
demonstration work in the person of my son Jack, who,
wrapped in a blanket, lay on a rug ready to be used as
my model. Twenty minutes after the lecture starts,
the door opens to admit a late-comer; shy, scared, and
speechless. I scold him soundly for his delay; thrust
a humerus into his hand, and impatiently recapitulate
for his benefit the lecture-notes which he has missed.
Once or twice, as the class proceeds, this late-comer
tries to speak; I quell him with a threatening glance,
and at length finish my lecture and dismiss the class.
The last-comer remains behind, presumably to
apologize; I administer a second strong dose of re-

proof, ending with: "Take yourself off now, and next time, remember, be here when the class begins!" To which the unfortunate wretch, articulating with great difficulty, replies: "Please, sir, I'm not a member of your class; I just came to say I have a terrible sore throat, and to ask what you could give me for it!"

Christmas Eve. A tragic Christmas this—all thought of seasonable gaiety obliterated by the Black Week through which the nation has just passed. Stormberg—Magersfontein—Colenso! The first reverse was a disappointment; the second, a disaster; the third, a tragedy. The nation is in mourning; everywhere men speak in tones of sorrow; a haunting gloom lies over this Border town, as over the whole Empire. Scotland mourns her Highland Brigade, the fine flower of the Army, so many of whom have followed their gallant leader, General Wauchope, to the other world. This brave officer, when bidding farewell to my brother George before embarking for South Africa, told him that he knew he would never return. My brother replied in effect: "Freits follow those who fear them" (the words of Sir Walter Scott to Mungo Park at a similar moment); the tragic sequence has been the same for this gallant soldier as it was for Sir Walter's intrepid friend.

Sorrowful days, these; a sorrowful year dragging out its life, uncheered by any ray of hope or comfort.

Dec. 31st. The last day of the year: and what is my day's record? Visited two charwomen; three widows; one baby with eleven brothers and sisters living on a labourer's wage; one spinster, self-supporting with the aid of a knitting-machine; and three members of the Ancient Order of Foresters, who remunerate me on a scale ranging from 1s. 10d. to 2s. 2d. per annum! Net result: for horse, man, self, and family—a day's labour = nothing.

Yet I cannot grudge it. It is little that one can do,

but one can do one's best, regarding whatever comes first to hand, and leave the rest alone. And for those who have not too many friends among mankind, one's best is never good enough. One often meets among them people with the finer feelings of human nature —occasionally, even, with gratitude! It is a grand privilege for a general practitioner to attend such cases, for he can thus follow the example of the great preaching Doctor, Jesus.

Jan. 1st, 1900. This New Year begins for Peebles with a Knighthood for Walter Thorburn, M.P., of Kerfield. All rejoice at this personal honour to one who has been a good member for all parties, also at the compliment conferred on the counties of Peebles and Selkirk.

Jan. 12th. Since 16th November my eldest brother, who has for twenty-one years been minister of Stichill, has been here under my care, very seriously ill. All this time he has been devotedly nursed by his mother and my wife; though suffering, and very weak, he has kept in closest touch with his parish, its interests and duties. In his pastoral letter at Christmas, written when desperately ill, he said: "I wish that this may be a Happy Christmas . . . it will be so in so far as we realize that 'whether we live or die, we are the Lord's.'"

To-day, here at Lindores (aged only forty-eight years), he passed to his rest: the most faithful minister I have ever known: the most loving of sons, the truest of brothers.

> There is no death! What seems so is transition;
> This life of mortal breath
> Is but a suburb of the life elysian
> Whose portal we call death.

April 1st. Yesterday, the thirteenth anniversary of our marriage, I had a strong presentiment of impending danger. So grave was this feeling that on being called out, at midnight, I purposely left beneath my pillow the gold watch bequeathed me by my brother George (given to him as a token of love from his parishioners, one year exactly before the day of his death, and deeply valued by me), ere setting forth on the journey to Manor Valley.

All went well at first, though the night was dark and starless, and the road difficult. I helped to add a new life to the cradle-roll of Manor parish; but on the return journey the smash duly arrived. Without warning, miles from home, my horse Peter came down with a sudden terrific crash. Kavanagh the coachman was shot clean over the horse's head; I was thrown out of the trap, landed on a steep bank, and rolled into the roadway. I picked myself up, unhurt; hauled the man to his feet, stunned; dressed his head, which was severely cut; and helped the horse to its legs again. It was now half-past one in the morning; in that lonely valley, no one was at hand to help. Then I heard the river singing on its way, and one by one the silent stars appeared. Now began the dismal tramp homeward. Lame and weary, we three "hunt-the-gowks" brought in All Fools' Day, footing the long miles down the valley. We reached home at 4.30 A.M., to find another maternity case awaiting me in the town. By 5.30 I was in bed; only to be knocked up once more at 6 to attend a man in delirium tremens! To-day, however, I managed to attend morning service in church, and gave thanks for preservation from the night's perils.

April 25th. To-day, Peebles has had a first-class thrill: the first Automobile Reliability Trials, which started two days ago from London to Edinburgh. Over eighty vehicles of all kinds entered for this spectacular event; to-day, in the course of about six hours, some fifty of these, which had survived, passed through Peebles amid the acclamations of its burgesses.

The shops were closed for the weekly half-day, so the entire population thronged the streets, like the Athenians, to see the "new thing" in progress.

Many of the strangely shaped vehicles, with their passengers, were so encrusted with dust, sand, and mud that they appeared to have emerged from the bottom of the sea rather than from a journey by dry land. Aboard several cars, ladies were alleged to have been espied; but as all the passengers wore bulky suits of leather, and were further disfigured by enormous helmets and observation spectacles with protruding rims, verification of sex was not easy.

These intrepid travellers resembled inhabitants of Mars on a visit to this planet, and were hailed as semi-miraculous beings by our Border folk; but no doubt, thirty years hence, they or their like will be circling above us in the air, flying from Edinburgh to London in a few hours, and, like Puck, "putting a girdle round the earth"!

April 29*th.* Two sad cases yesterday. Examined a man far gone in alcoholic lunacy, who had dug a grave in his house, with the express intention of burying one of his children in it; whether alive or dead it was not clear. The second case was even more tragic: a young couple, one week married, spending their honeymoon in Peebles. I was called in to find the bride, in all her wedding finery, evidently *in extremis*. Nothing whatever could be done; at eight o'clock this morning she died, after one brief week of wedded happiness—the burnished new wedding-ring on her finger, her bracelets still on her arms, her bridal finery scattered about the room. I asked the minister to go and comfort the poor stunned husband; this he did immediately, though it was Communion Sunday, visiting him between the two dispensations of the Sacrament. My wife also went, and laid flowers on the coffin. Two thoughts came to me, with the power to speak them to the husband as I shook his hand at parting. Firstly, that they had together shared supreme bliss on earth, though only for one brief week, and that the memory of this would be a radiant dream all his life long. Secondly, Tennyson's words:

> I hold it true whate'er befall,
> I feel it when I sorrow most,
> 'Tis better to have loved and lost
> Than never to have loved at all.

May 11*th*. An adventurous day. To-night I rode my newly purchased motor-tricycle (to replace my old horse, which, after many years of devoted service, is now past his work) from Edinburgh to Peebles— my first experience on such a steed!

Preparatory to this somewhat daring experiment, I had insured myself to the amount of £3000, so that in case of death by motor-accident, my heirs would be consoled to that amount. I had also instructed my wife, in case I did not return, to ring up the Infirmary, or, alternatively, the Police. The engine (a de Dion, 2¼ horse-power) felt like a wild animal beneath me, eager to bolt, and needing to be held in with might and main. One would require three hands and six senses wherewith to master and manage it; steering-gear, brake, trumpet, and electric spark, with four additional levers—all to be controlled while running at top speed. One has to have eyes at the back of one's head, and on all sides at once, in order to avoid running down a bailie or a bairn. The ubiquitous policeman, too, has to be watched for, as he lies in wait, note-book in hand, to seize the luckless rider exceeding the regulation speed, or travelling without a light after dusk.

I started at 7 P.M., by Morningside, Tollcross, and out *via* the Braid Hills towards open country. All along the route much interest was aroused by the machine, these motors having not yet become common, as they assuredly will one day. Urchins ran behind, commenting freely and loudly; at Penicuik Brae— a tough proposition—some of these (when I paused, breathless) expressed gleeful willingness to shove behind. The de Dion, however, did not require their aid, but took the hill in her stride, and by 9.15 P.M. we were scorching up the ascent of Peebles Old Town in expert style. My children, warned by the trumpet, which spoke with no uncertain voice, and by the thunder of the engine, sprang from bed and rushed in their nightgowns into the street. My wife and the servants followed, and the whole household received the adventurer with acclamation, to the strains of *Hail to the Chief!*

I am in hopes that this new method of transport will enable me to work the practice at less expense than with man, horse, and trap, as some retrenchment is necessary with a view to educating the children.

May 13*th.* Ever since I came to live in Peebles I have been strangely fascinated by the spectacle of the historic Cross Kirk in its ruined and abandoned condition. Within its walls much of the burgh's history has been enacted. In mediæval times, religious teaching and physical healing flowed from it, as from a fountain, to town and country-side; its charity and succour extended to fellow-countrymen in misfortune abroad—an early sowing in the "foreign mission field"!

Holy Fairs were held within its precincts, when pilgrims, convoyed thither by repentance and hope, found the weary homeward miles lightened by absolution and consolation. The Stuart Kings not only contributed to its revenues, but came as pilgrims to its shrine and made their orisons at its altars. To the young Borderers of to-day, the Cross Kirk ought surely to appeal as romance rekindled by tradition; to the middle-aged, as the palladium of those liberties so dearly won by their forefathers; to the old, as a symbol of that peace and beauty which should mark the close of a life well spent.

Yet what is the Cross Kirk to-day? An abomination of desolation — overgrown with weeds, buried in rubbish, encumbered with nettles, hemlock, and mounds of earth. The walls totter to their destruction; a hideous hen-house is propped against the Norman tower; the trees are unsightly through decay and neglect. A rubble dyke fences the precincts, but cannot conceal the shameful state into which this ancient holy house has been allowed, through apathy and materialism, to fall.

Three years ago I pleaded with the Town Council to make the restoration and preservation of the place a feature of the Diamond Jubilee commemoration; but nothing was done. Had I the money, I would myself "bell the cat" by starting on excavating and levelling work forthwith; but I have not the means. However, I will not despair, but continue, in season and out, to urge on the work; who knows but, in the end, " *contra nando incrementum*"? There may one day be increase; but the tide of apathy sets strongly against one's hopes.

May 16*th.* A picture in the National Gallery, which bears the title *Leaving the Manse*, sums up to-day's doings. My wife and I, with my mother and the other members of the family, to-day took leave of Stichill Manse, the place which my brother George had taught us, during his twenty-one years' ministry there, to look upon as home. For the last time we sat round its hospitable table, his place vacant. The garden was, as ever, lovely, though rifled of its wealth of daffodils and other spring flowers, which had been given to the villagers; his Alpine rockery, with its fifteen hundred species, had been cleared. The fruit-trees bowed beneath their load of bloom; the laburnum branches drooped in golden clusters over the seat where we had so often talked together.

Late in the afternoon we drove away, each one wrapped in thought, in memory, and in regret. The day was beautiful, and Nature at her loveliest; our memories of Stichill Manse will be of a place radiant with sunshine, fragrant with blossom, alive with singing birds, and surrounded by the breath of heaven.

May 18*th*. At 9.30 this evening we heard by telephone the news that Mafeking has at last been relieved. After seven months' siege, one had dreaded that, as in Gordon's case at Khartoum, relief might come just too late. Baden-Powell—self-reliant, self-controlled, self-effacing—has been in no small degree the genius of this beleaguered village on the veldt. A great weight is lifted from men's hearts, here and throughout the Queen's Dominions.

August 15*th*. I enjoyed a talk to-day with an old friend who was visiting the town. He is a "dominie" of the older persuasion, which flourished before the days of School Boards and mass methods in education. He had a great flair for individualizing and discriminating among his pupils, and for detecting and fostering any likely "lad o' pairts": such specializing is much less frequent nowadays, when a master has to force on every pupil to one dead level of examination-tests.

November 23*rd*. The memorial volume to my eldest brother, on which I have been engaged since his death last January, is now in the press. I have been encouraged in the labour of preparing it by the conviction that such men as he can influence and stimulate others from beyond the grave. It is therefore one's duty to publish, if the material exists, some record of their struggles, labours, and thoughts, so that others, reading these, may be heartened for the daily "warstle" with fate and life. This book, like all my writings, has been planned and carried through under a cloud of acute discouragement. But I console myself with the reflection that were it not for my scribbling I should perish of monotony amid the "small beer" of a country town!

December 6th. To-day, in a comely young wife whom I was attending, I noticed the most beautiful set of regular and perfect teeth I had ever come across in practice. I questioned her as to sweet-eating, in which she indulges freely; as to porridge, which she never touches; as to tea, which she drinks very hot and very strong! Finally, determined to probe the secret, I asked: "What do you brush your teeth with?" "Nothing, Doctor; I never brush them at all!" Every rule of dental hygiene has been recklessly broken by this intrepid young woman; yet the results are excellent. The secret of dental preservation and decay, one infers, lies deeper than the rules, and certainly far beyond the cult of "toothbrush drill."

December 9th. In the small hours this morning, a countryman from Harrow-Hope arrived to summon me to attend his wife. He was the first to "hansel" the new speaking-tube at the patients' entrance, which I had installed in our new house to save myself from night exposure (my nocturnal conversations having up to now resembled the Balcony Scene from *Romeo and Juliet*, conducted from an open window). I shouted directions down the tube, at first vainly; the visitor was so scared by the new-fangled apparatus, and by the uncanny sound of my voice at his ear in the darkness, where he could see no one, that he remained obstinately mute. At length, however, I prevailed on him to speak into the tube, when the following duologue ensued:

"Doctor, I'm needin' ye for my wife."

"And who, then, is your wife?"

"'Deed, ye ken fine wha she is, Doctor; ye promised ye wad come!"

"Yes, yes; but what is your name? Where do you come from?"

(Loud outburst of derisive laughter, then)

"Hoots, Doctor, ye ken me fine, it's juist masel', ye ken; come awa' noo, come awa'!"

"Save us, man, how can I come if you won't tell me who you are or where to come to?"

(Louder explosion of laughter, then)

"Och, Doctor, I hae it noo, an' I'm sure I beg your pardon: I'm the shepherd frae the Harrow-Hope, that's wha I am! Wull ye come noo, Doctor?"

This messenger, on returning to his native glen, spread far and wide a graphic account of the supernatural invention he had encountered; the tale became a household word in his remote parish for many years.

December 15*th*. This morning at 2.30 I bicycled through a gale of wind and rain to a maternity case at Easter Dawyck. Dismounting at a farm-steading (the track ahead being impossible for riding) I sought an outhouse in which to leave my cycle; all doors, at that early hour, were closely bolted and barred. I therefore wheeled the machine across the haugh above the river bank, and deposited it in a likely "bield." Then, on foot, over the bridge, across the hilly land to my destination, where I was detained for some time.

Back once more through wind and rain—where is the bicycle? No sign of it anywhere. At length, by the light of a pocket electric-lamp, I located the machine in midstream, half-submerged by the rapidly rising river, which had flooded the haugh and carried it away. Nothing for it but to wade into Tweed, up to the knees, and rescue the ill-starred bicycle from a watery grave. This I did, aided by the electric-lamp (the cycle-lamp was of course past praying for), and, despite the raging stream and howling wind, successfully salved my steed and rode homewards, reaching Lindores at 7.30 A.M., the gale at my back pushing me on faster than, owing to the heavy roads and wintry darkness, I could otherwise have hoped.

December 31*st* (*Hogmanay*). The year and the century have but a few hours more to run. I have much to be grateful for in home and family; the practice too has improved in quality during the twelve-month, and I feel myself established in the confidence of the people. For the many mercies vouchsafed during this year, and for the memory of my eldest brother, which is now my deepest inspiration, I thank God and take courage.

January 22nd, 1901. This evening at 7.30 the telephone bell rang, to announce the news of the Queen's death at Osborne. Since Sunday, the nation has held its breath, dreading this blow; now that it is upon them, men are stunned. Two generations have known no other Queen; her people feel strangely orphaned and bereft. One had scarcely realized that the Queen was mortal; that age and death must have their way, even with a monarch. Our minister, Matthew Gardner, tells me he intends to preach his memorial sermon from the text, "As one that mourneth for his mother," which seems to me both apt and striking. Shakespeare's lines ring in my mind to-night:

> Fear no more the heat o' the sun,
> Nor the furious winter's rages. . . .
> . . . Quiet consummation have,
> And renowned be thy grave.

January 29th. This week I have had the good fortune to meet, at Kingsmeadows House, three distinguished and stimulating men: my host, Andrew Stewart, LL.D., founder of the Chair of Political Economy at Glasgow University; General Ritchie, an Indian Mutiny veteran; and Sir William Arrol, builder of the Forth Bridge. My host told me that in the original designs for the Bridge, for which Arrol was not responsible, a serious miscalculation occurred. This Arrol detected, and pointed out to those in charge that, were the design adopted, the Bridge would stand neither the vertical nor the lateral strain involved.

"Then," was the reply, "tear up the design and build according to your own; we can trust you."

Arrol did so; the plans were altered, the strains re-calculated; he added his own percentage to the expenses, and the Bridge was successfully built.

To meet such men as these, each having essayed and achieved so much, solely by his own efforts and despite adverse circumstances, is in itself a liberal education.

January 30th. I have lately been prescribing paraffin internally to an aged patient unaware of its con-stituents. To-day however, on visiting his house, I was confronted by a bottle sent by the chemist, plainly labelled "Superfine Paraffin." The patient's sister held it up with the accusing query: "Did ye order oor John paraffin?" On my reluctantly admitting the crime, she replied with a disdainful sniff: "Had I kent that, I wad hae gie'd him a drap oot o' the lamp an' saved the expense!"

March 13th. This morning I had a sorrowful task. A rural postman passes my front gate daily at the same hour; his wife, whom I sent lately to Edinburgh Infirmary, has been given fifteen months to live. To-day I had to hand him the letter announcing the Professor's verdict, for which he was completely un-prepared. I waited for him in the clear sunshine of a morning like midsummer; the birds sang at their nest-building, and the air was warm and sweet. He greeted me, as usual, with a cheery laugh; I handed him the letter. When he came to the words "not more than fifteen months to live," he crushed it in his hand with a great sob, and trudged heavily away without a word. The sunshine seemed a mockery in face of such unavailing sorrow.

March 17th. Talking with the minister to-night, I brought up the ancient theological "hair-splitter" dear to the mediæval schoolmen: "How many angels can be supported on the point of a needle?" He replied: "A friend of mine once settled that for good and all. The answer is, seven. He led his questioners to a certain poor home in his parish, the window of which was lighted, but unshuttered. 'What do you see?' 'A woman with seven bairns about her, sewing for dear life.' 'That woman is a widow, and penniless; these seven angels (in embryo) are supported on the point of her needle. Q.E.D.'"

March 28th. Yesterday a middle-aged woman suffering from spinal curvature, for whom I had ordered a week's rest in bed, refused point-blank to comply on the grounds that she cannot afford rest. She grinds out a living by knitting socks and stockings on a machine, at the rate of 4d. and 5d. per pair. I could not argue against so cogent a reason; but leaving her at the machine, visited four of her neighbours in quick succession. "Will you see to Miss M——'s fire daily for one week?" "Will you give her breakfast (or tea, or dinner) for one week?" All consented at once, ungrudgingly. Then to my friend the LL.D. at Kingsmeadows, who at once sent a pound-note anonymously by post, to cover the loss on the stocking-knitting. To-day the patient lies in bed, at ease in mind and body; a good fire blazes, and meals appear as if by magic, punctually and in rotation. I noted various small touches, too, of care and attention, added by the neighbours over and above the letter of the contract; such refresh one's often jaded belief in the inherent decency and generosity of human nature.

April 28th (Sunday). This afternoon I attended a Confirmation Service in the Roman Catholic Church here, at which the Archbishop of St Andrews and Edinburgh was the Celebrant. The church stands hard by the ruined Cross Kirk. It was strangely touching to hear the ancient Latin prayers and the beautiful traditional hymns in the same tongue, chanted once more as in pre-Reformation days they must often have echoed through its precincts. "Bare, ruined choirs, where late the sweet birds sang," describes them best to-day.

July 19*th*. To-day the Celtic Cross erected to the memory of my brother George by his parishioners was unveiled at Stichill by Sir George Douglas. My wife and I and the three elder children were present, with the other members of the family; my mother was absent in body, owing to ill-health. There was a large gathering, among them many unforgotten faces; but one missed the one generous, large-hearted personality which bound us all together in remembrance. The oration—brief, beautiful, poetic—was profoundly moving. The words on the Cross are these (from the Book of Daniel): "A man greatly beloved." They include everything one thinks and feels to-day—his achievement, his memorial, our heritage. One would give a lifetime of service to have these words written above one at the end.[1]

August 18*th* (*Sunday*). This morning Mr Gardner preached a powerful practical sermon which will have far-reaching results. The common lodging-house in the Long Close, which is the plague-spot of Peebles, supplied him with a text made to his hand. During the week he had been summoned there to visit an infant of twenty months, whose mother, a vagrant, is lying in the Calton Jail, Edinburgh, for twenty-one days. The child, fit and well on entering the lodging-house, was there fed mainly on whisky; it sickened and died. This tragedy fired the minister's imagination, and re-acted in turn on his hearers; when the sermon ended, many flocked to the vestry to offer sums of money wherewith to build a model lodging-house. One such offer was for £1000. A meeting is to be held to con-sider the situation and to provide a sound financial basis for the scheme. Matters will be by no means easy to arrange, since vested interests are against the scheme, and the *vis inertiæ* in certain quarters a potent

[1] On the Celtic Cross which marks the grave of Dr Gunn in Peebles Churchyard these same words are inscribed [ED.].

obstruction; but the first stone has thus been laid, and better things will result. The frail, fugitive breath of a dead infant has fulfilled its appointed task, ere taking flight from the Long Close to happier lands.

September 29*th.* We returned yesterday from a month's holiday—a fortnight spent with our four children in Edinburgh, and the remainder *à deux*, my wife and self, in the north and west. It has been an invigorating and happy experience, rarely possible for a hard-wrought doctor to enjoy. With the children, I renewed early recollections of "mine own romantic town," and found it more engrossing than ever, if that could be. Then, as staid married folks, my wife and I revisited Newburgh and Lindores Abbey, with their golden memories of former days; and once more enjoyed the famous pears, which were conveniently in season. A visit to Iona— for long my most cherished project—crowned our adventures with the glory of a dream fulfilled. At Oban we encountered stormy weather, and were reminded of the perilous passage in an open boat shared by the famous Dr Norman Macleod and another minister. So acute was the danger, that it was suggested that one of the ministers should pray. The boatman, glancing from the strong, stalwart Macleod to his smaller-built professional brother, replied: "The wee minister can pray if he likes, but the big yin maun tak' an oar!"

September 30*th.* My wife visited an ailing neighbour to-day and inquired whether the family had had a holiday this year. The answer was: "We never take a holiday. When we tire of the kitchen, we move into 'the room' for a few weeks and make believe we have 'flitted.' Then when winter comes, we 'flit' back to the kitchen and enjoy it all the better for the change." I foresee—and have had pleasure in pointing out—that this inexpensive holiday programme will probably, willy-nilly, be ours next year!

November 16*th*. This morning I was called out at four o'clock—a bitter frosty dawn, with snow-coated roads. On my way back from the maternity case, some miles away, to which I had been summoned, I was conscious as I cycled along the dark solitary highway, of a sudden sense of happiness, well-being, and freedom. Half-an-hour after reaching home, I was handed a telegram announcing my mother's death. It had taken place at half-past six, precisely at the moment when I had experienced the sense of benediction and of peace. Her spirit, I believe, touched mine in passing.

November 19*th*. To-day we laid my mother's body in its last resting-place. A solemn, sorrowful task— yet soon accomplished. I am now back at home, and at work—the one anodyne for such sorrow. Yet in mind I feel sorely lonely, and in spirit no longer a boy, now she is gone. She has tholed forty years of widowhood; brought up her family single-handed and well; guided her life by self-denial, courage, and a Godgiven sense of right. Never once, in all these years, has she compromised with any wrong action or ignoble standard. All this, realized to-night as never before, brings me some comfort. One can thank God for such a mother. With her spirit, and that of George my brother, may I be granted life-long communion. But would that she were back here beside me, and I once more a boy again!

January 28*th*, 1902. To-day I have travelled, by train and cycle, 55 miles to visit four patients! This breaks all my previous records save one—66 miles for three visits. Such toilsome journeys not only consume one's working day, but exhaust one's energy; yet in a sparsely populated county, with a widely scattered practice, they are unavoidable. During this month of January I have had no fewer than sixteen nights in the open—long journeys, severe weather, and difficult cases. Small wonder that Mungo Park preferred to return to the wilds of Africa rather than to endure practising medicine for another winter in the wilds of Peeblesshire!

March 12th. To-night the minister and his wife, with two other couples, dined with us; a pleasant oasis in a crowded day, which began for me with a country journey at 2 A.M. My wife had provided excellent fare; we were "all well content and merry," as Pepys would say. The minister was delighted when informed that Irene (aged not quite four), who is a devoted churchgoer, inquired loudly, last Sunday, in the hearing of the congregation, the instant after he had given out the Blessing: "What's the Sunday pudding to be?"

Alas, at 9 P.M. a summons came from St Gordian's, miles away in Manor Valley; no help for it but to leave the merry party in full swing. 'Twas ever thus —and as like as not, a false alarm at the end of it! One feels on such occasions like the man in St Matthew's Gospel: "He said, 'I will not,' . . . and went"—a fitting epitaph for many a country doctor! How often, thus inopportunely summoned, have I sat, "weary and ill at ease" in conscience, debating the alternatives: if I go, it will be yet another case of "Wolf! Wolf!"; if I don't, it may be acute appendicitis! Having reiterated, "I will not!" loud enough to disturb the family circle, though not to drown the voice of conscience, one always repents and goes in the end—often to find a slight colic attack as the reward of virtue!

April 22nd. I visited to-day an old woman of eighty-two who was in her day one of the most notable spinners in the country-side. A talk with her is like a dip into Galt's *Annals of the Parish*, where he speaks of "the booming of the meikle wheel (to make blankets) and the birring of the little wheel for sheets and napery," which under that industrious bee, the second Mrs Balwhidder, made the manse resound for many a day "like an organ kist." My old "spinster" patient confessed that she was "no great hand at the little wheel" all her days; but for the big wheel she would collect from the slopes of Cademuirhill, on summer evenings, as much sheep's wool as would, when spun, carded, dyed, and woven, make three pairs of blankets, or three suits of clothing for her sons. She has lived a long hard life, mainly on cold porridge, which is in her opinion the secret of health and of survival.

This morning, very early, I saw the first swallow flying across Tweed. To-night, with my young son George, I forsook the Burgh Records for a plunge into the *Iliad*, which he is now promoted to study, but which I relish somewhat better than he does at this stage.

May 31*st*. To-night the whole nation has but one question, "Is it Peace?" The time-limit for the Boers' acceptance or rejection of our terms expires to-day. One grieves to look back on the strain, sacrifice, sorrow, and loss which this war of over two and a half years has involved; may to-morrow bring not merely "ease after warre," but a firm enduring peace to both adversaries who have fought so bravely.

June 1*st* (*Sunday*). Peace has come at last. A telegram arrived from the Scottish Office announcing the glad tidings; and at 8.50 this evening, from the Parish Kirk steeple, the bell rang out its rejoicing peal. Crowds thronged the streets, and one heard on all sides the heartfelt prayer: "Thank God for peace!"

June 7*th*. One awakes daily now with a feeling of intense relief; peace has come. I find myself doing my rounds with a light heart, and meet rejoicing and thankfulness in every house I visit. Our children are using the banners, bunting, and fireworks with which we celebrated war victories, to welcome the greatest achievement of all—the consummation of these dark sorrowful years. An editor whom I met to-day tells me that the war-correspondents have exercised much ingenuity in conveying their forecasts of an early peace to their respective newspapers by means of cypher cables. One of these, received on 12th April, ran: "Regarding purchase Paxfontein gold-mine, all necessary parties to contract now Pretoria, whither Alf gone get better price. Every reason to believe vendors have wish sell." (Here "Paxfontein" = Peace; "Alf" = Lord Milner; "vendors = "the Boers.) A later cable, the terms of which had been previously agreed on, ran: "Have bought 1000 Rand Collieries 40s. 6d." This, interpreted, meant "Peace absolutely assured." Yet another correspondent cabled, in default of a pre-arranged signal, "Whitsuntide Greetings," and timed his message to arrive on Whit-Monday. When the Gospel for the day was consulted, the words "Peace I leave with you" at once supplied the clue.

June 14th. This afternoon we combined two commemorations in a family festival: the coming of peace, and the birthday of our elder boy, George—the latter celebration having been postponed on account of inclement weather. Peggy and I spread the picnic feast by Manor Water, and the children, with their friends, gathered bouquets of marsh-marigolds, lilac, hawthorn, and forget-me-not to adorn the scene. Close by was the beautiful avenue of trees leading to Barns House—a Gothic cathedral two miles long, with its trembling firmament of sun-pierced foliage. The June leaves (lime, beech, plane, ash, and oak) were exquisitely fresh and green; their fragrance in the hot sunshine filled the air. Swallows were skimming swiftly in and out of an old weather-beaten barn near by, and from its rafters came the soft "cheep-cheeping" of their young. Afterwards the children played cricket and other games. We seemed to dwell for a space "in a land where it was always afternoon," with the dark winter of the war days behind us, and summer, youth, and happiness around.

June 24th. The Coronation is postponed on account of the King's sudden and serious illness. The disease is diagnosed as perityphlitis, and the King was operated upon at noon to-day; no bulletins issued as yet. This grave news spells consternation everywhere. It reached us here during the afternoon; my wife was just leaving the house when two Coronation flags hoisted by the children above the front gate fell suddenly at her feet. As she bent to pick them up, a neighbour dashed in with the bad news. We hastily removed all our bunting, and the flags are being withdrawn from the church tower and public buildings. It looks as though no Coronation could be possible for at least two or three months; temporary paralysis of trade is certain to result, as so many industries have been involved in the gigantic preparations for the event.

Another tragedy appears in this evening's papers: my friend Colonel Ivison Macadam has been murdered in his laboratory by a madman.

July 18th, 1902. Four nights ago a vagrant came to interview me—one of thirty such during the past month. All he possessed being the sum of half-a-crown, he obtained advice free. To-night he reappeared in my consulting-room. Expecting a demand for some further benefit, such as admission to the Poorhouse, I assumed the firm cautious air usually needful for such cases, most of whom are drunkards, idlers, and impostors. To my surprise he said: "Sure, sir, after doing what you told me, I'm quite myself again, so I came in just to thank you."

Among the hundreds of tramps whom I have attended and prescribed for, this wandering Irishman is the only one who has ever returned to say "thank you." I was reminded of the Gospel incident of the ten cleansed lepers: "Where are the nine?"

August 6th. To-day I had the curious experience, rare in a country town, of attending in rotation two German ladies of the most pronounced rationalist belief (or unbelief); an aristocratic Roman Catholic family, ultra-devout in doctrine and practice; and the Very Reverend Professor Charteris, an evangelical believer and worker of good works. Such contrasted, positive, and enthusiastic tenets, firmly held, and reflected in conversation, give one furiously to think.

August 10th. To-day being the long-deferred Coronation Sunday, rejoicings were expressed in church, and echoed by us all, in the words of the 21st Psalm: "(The King) asked life of thee, and thou gavest it him . . . thou settest a crown of pure gold on his head."

Last night my wife and I were guests at a Coronation dinner held at the Hydropathic—a gay and brilliant scene, where the King's health was proposed by Captain Warren, of the battleship *Undaunted*. Up to the very last moment, superstitious apprehensions persisted that the postponed Coronation would not take place without disaster; but all is now happily accomplished, to the tune of "Vive le Roi!"

November 29th. To-day my volume of one hundred sonnets, composed during the past nine years, is published under the title of *A Doctor's Thoughts*. In my own opinion, these verses are but crude reflections of the varying emotions and events of a doctor's life, valuable only for the sincerity with which they are set down. But the writing of them has whiled away the hours of many a nocturnal vigil, and shortened many a tedious journey along the hilly roads and lonely valleys of Tweeddale. We shall see how they are received by the public. Blessed are they that expect nothing, for they shall not be disappointed!

I have to-day presented the first copy of the book to my wife, and posted the second to Winifred, now at boarding-school in Edinburgh. I miss sorely the pleasure of presenting a copy to my mother, as I had hoped to do; her sympathetic encouragement, and that of my brother George, were ever precious to me in all my literary efforts, and heartened me to persevere.

December 14th (Sunday). I have had for once a quiet restful day, of which, after several heavy weeks of winter work, I felt greatly in need. As we sat by the fireside, with a violent tempest of hail and wind howling without, Win (home for the holidays) peppered us with my Sonnets, knowing well that the rest of the family could not escape! Needless to say, their author was their sternest critic. The first reviews of the book are now to hand—surprisingly good. We await the remainder, however, with trepidation.

During the night I was called out to Stobo. My man drove me there through a terrific onslaught of snow, hail, and wind. Great flashes of wildfire flared at intervals through the driving snow, like naphtha-lamps at a country fair: a sinister freak of nature's fancy, which daunted both man and beast in some degree.

New Year's Day, 1903. For our poor children's party, to-day, we found at the last minute that the invited guests numbered thirteen. This seemed inauspicious for a New Year's feast, so out I went to secure an addition. At the gate I ran into a ragged urchin who inquired: "Please, Doctor, how much is it to get in to the party to-night?" I led him indoors forthwith as Number Fourteen; and very merry we were, with a Christmas Tree and all the seasonable games. Our four children sang, danced, and recited for their guests' amusement; one of the urchins, a tiny girl aged six, spurred on by the force of example, volunteered to recite also. She then declaimed the whole of the Second Paraphrase, slowly and expressionlessly, but without a mistake, to the great edification of the company.

January 3rd. I visited to-day Mrs Watt, a sister of the late Sheriff Hunter. This lady's husband, now dead, was Auditor of the Court of Session, and possessed numerous autograph letters from Sir Walter Scott, Carlyle, Jeffrey, Brougham, Coleridge, Leigh Hunt, and others. One of Sir Walter's (hitherto unpublished) which was shown me, is addressed to a young poet named Stewart, then lying in prison awaiting the death-penalty for some unspecified crime. He had sent Sir Walter a collection of his poems, with the pitiful request that the author of *Waverley* would intercede with the King on his behalf. Scott's reply —one of the manliest, kindest, and most compassionate he ever wrote—informs the doomed man that he has done everything possible to save him, but, he fears, in vain. In simple, moving words he counsels the poor lad to prepare for the great change which lies before him; holds out no false hope, but gravely indicates the path of peace. Young Stewart was ultimately hanged.[1]

As I read this letter I recalled a startling incident related to me by the manager of the Edinburgh Life Assurance Company, who, while filling up a proposal form for a prospective client, put the usual question, "What did your father die of?" and received the terse reply, "He was hanged!"

February 23rd. To-night I was sent for in great haste to certify a young man suffering, as it turned out, from homicidal mania. On entering the house I had at once to dodge a small solid stool hurled with terrific force at my head. The patient, a finely built, handsome and athletic young man, persistently

---

[1] Lockhart states that the sentence was commuted to transportation for life [ED.]

directed his worst attacks at me, ignoring the three men whom I commandeered to assist me. He hurled kettles, a poker, chairs, and ornaments at me in turn, and fought desperately with the superhuman strength common in such cases. When at length, by united exertions, the four of us succeeded in pinning him down on the floor so as to secure his limbs, he shouted: "I have instructions from the Lord Jesus Christ to murder Dr Gunn!" This intention was eventually foiled by two constables, with whose help we finally secured and handcuffed the poor creature, who was thereupon taken straight to the asylum at Rosewell. (Later. He subsequently died there of acute mania.)

March 22nd (Sunday). To-day we embark on an untried adventure in theology. For twenty-eight successive Sundays, we are to sample as many different preachers, most of them well-known leaders in the Church. Our own minister, Matthew Gardner, sailed for South Africa yesterday, with leave of absence for four months. How will matters stand on his return? Shall we then be Laodiceans, Antinomians, Erastians, Latitudinarians, or still what "Pet Marjorie" termed "Presbitterans"? I wonder. We are about to receive the truth in twenty-eight varying guises; will it still remain truth when our education is accomplished? The coming months will provide great temptations for the weaker vessels to "wander," and for the unregenerate to forsake churchgoing altogether! Either course is deemed a disgrace, as witness the characteristic remark of an old wheelwright at an election meeting here some years ago. Sir Charles Tennant was being severely heckled, and as one questioner rose to his feet, the wheelwright shouted from the back of the hall: "Dinna answer thon yin, Chairlie; *he* gangs to nae kirk!" A second heckler rushed into the breach, and again the warning rang out: "Dinna answer thon yin either, Chairlie; *he* gangs to twa kirks!"

March 29*th*. Everyone is saddened by the suicide of the gallant Hector Macdonald—"Fighting Mac," whose heroic name became a household word during the recent dark years of war. Now his light has been put out while it is yet day, and by his own hand! A bright torch quenched in a muddy pool. When all is said, his was a gallant soul—"*sans peur*," if not "*sans reproche*."

April 3*rd*. Three days ago I discovered that a woman suffering acutely from bronchitis persists daily in polishing, to a supreme degree of brilliance, the brass name-plate on her garden gate. This task, which she has elevated into a religious rite, exposes her to the piercing winds now prevalent, and aggravates her trouble; so I forbade its continuance. Her ultimatum was: "Well, Doctor, I'll get my man to take off the plate, and then I can still polish it here!" To-day I found the brass plate, radiating lustre, duly installed on the mantelpiece of the "best room." So much for the mentality of Martha *in excelsis*!

May 12*th*. To-day (as Surgeon-captain in the Royal Scots), I attended the Royal Levee at the Palace of Holyroodhouse—the first held there by King Edward. We duly assembled in the picture gallery, where the Royal Archers in their picturesque green uniforms and Glengarry caps, each man holding a six-foot bow and three arrows, added a vivid touch of colour to the already brilliant scene. On approaching the gold-and-scarlet Throne, one's name having been announced by the Lord Chamberlain, one distinctly felt that one was in the presence of no regal nonentity, but of a vigorous and forceful personality. The King's heavy-lidded eyes held little or no expression; his head inclined automatically as each fresh presentation was made, while his body remained immobile. Nevertheless the brief encounter revealed him not as a figure-head, but as a man, and a man to be reckoned with.

May 14*th*. A few days ago, in *The Scotsman*, I advertised orphaned twin boys "for disposal," and received forty-five replies! All the applicants demanded a premium, save one, whose letter arrived too late for consideration, as I had succeeded meanwhile in placing the twins locally, though in separate homes. Each of these hard-working mothers, with slender means but a rich heart, has adopted an orphan for nothing.

June 4th. Yesterday I amputated the leg of an old man of seventy-five, one of the bravest patients I have ever had. As he was about to take the anæsthetic, he observed with a chuckle, "Eh, Doctor, ye're a graun' lad!" and then shouted to his daughter in the next room: "Jenny, lass, awa' an' seek a box for the doctor to pit the leg in!" To-day, when I called, I found him as serenely unconcerned as though nothing had happened; he told me that he had slept all night and now felt "gey weel"; but was very wroth when I refused him permission to sit on a chair at the open door to enjoy the sunshine! There are few such Stoics left among us.

June 12th. At present I am enjoying the congenial society of Dr Hay Fleming, the eminent Scottish historian; we have many things in common. His encouraging interest in the Presbytery Records which I am transcribing—*nulla dies sine linea*—has fanned the flame of my enthusiasm, which oft-times wanes under the monotony of the task. I am sometimes sorely tempted to exclaim "*Cui bono?*" But the companionship of a fellow-enthusiast is a powerful stimulus. Besides, but for the nepenthe of oblivion which my literary vices yield me, I should often find the daily round well-nigh insupportable.

To-day I met a child carrying flowers, and on asking, "What have you got there?" received the instant response, "The lesser ranunculus!" Plain buttercups are evidently frowned upon by our modern botanical professors in the schools.

This morning we tholed an interminable discourse upon the sluggard, from a visiting minister who in appearance resembled his subject to the life, being fat, ponderous, slow of speech and indolent in manner. He might have illustrated his text, as Faed the artist once did, from a derelict farm-steading near the hamlet of Lyne, a few miles away. For years this farm was no better than a picturesque ruin, its thatch tied on with rotten ropes, and further secured by broken ladders; pigs and hens ran freely in and out of the dwelling-house; neglect, procrastination and confusion reigned. The presiding genius of the place was always to be seen, hands in pockets—placid, good-natured and bone-lazy.

July 10*th*. For the last ten days I have been suffering from acute sciatica, which has left me weak and nervously exhausted. I derived some benefit—in the form of a counter-irritant—from various Job's comforters among the friends who visited me. Their lugubrious consolations provoked me to bad language, and thus momentarily distracted my mind from my sufferings!

Yesterday an original Sunday-school treat was arranged by the Rev. John Cruickshank, minister of Stobo, when the children of his parish were conveyed here *en masse* and attended Sanger's Circus. This joy of joys, to the child-heart, will long be a glory to look back upon, though the "unco guid" will probably wag their heads! Once more the second "gude and gentle Stobo," as we affectionately call him, has justified his title.

The common lodging-house in the Long Close, anent which discussion has raged ever since the Sunday when it furnished the Church Militant with a battle-cry, has now been closed down, thoroughly cleansed, and gutted of its insanitary abuses. This is a necessary stepping-stone to further constructive action; on the minister's return from abroad, it is hoped to erect a new building to replace the old. Meanwhile the vagrants, deprived of their casual sheltering home, sleep out-of-doors throughout the country-side; in this halcyon summer weather little harm results. The Long Close now stands empty and unregretted; already the swallows nest in its rafters, and only sunbeams sleep within its derelict walls.

August 27th. To-night I took my wife to hear the famous entertainer, George Grossmith; but alas, was disappointed in him. I fear I am losing the faculty of mirth. One incident, however, has made me laugh to-day. A woman with a trifling ailment, whom I told through the speaking-tube to go to a junior doctor, roused me again from slumber, fully an hour later, with the plaintive question: "Please, sir, what *is* a junior doctor?" Needless to add, I undertook the case.

March 19th, 1904. Some time ago, when leaving Peebles by train for a country visit, I observed a comely middle-aged woman standing at the door of one of the railway cottages, waving her hand to the driver of our train. To-day, while I was attending her, she told me that for forty years she had thus waved her husband God-speed, every time he drove a train out of the station. At nights, she makes her signal with a lantern; she has never once missed in all these many years. Such fidelity in small things is as refreshing as it is rare.

June 24th (Beltane Day). A day of vivid contrasts. The town has been *en fête* from early morning onwards; all the ancient ceremonial of Riding the Marches, Crowning the Queen, and so forth, being duly observed. Dr Hay Fleming, who spent the afternoon with us, was much diverted by these picturesque survivals from an older age. Together from the windows of this house, we watched the gaily dressed crowds wend their way towards the merrymaking, and he egged me on to quote the appropriate stanzas from King James's *Peblis to the Play*. We saw "Hope Kailzie and Cardrona gathered out thickfold," and from the opposite quarter, "all the wenches of the west" appeared to have forgathered also!

Later, we two antiquarians withdrew to my consulting room, and became engrossed in the deciphering and transcription of an ancient document. Sounds of revelry and festal music reached us from time to time; but like Sir Walter's Monkbarns, we two dryasdusts found the sleeping past more enthralling than the waking present.

Our zealous labours were interrupted by an urgent summons for me—an accident case on the railway. Hastily collecting stretchers and coverings, I drove to the spot, a couple of miles distant, to find that one of the merrymakers, while trespassing on the line, had been killed outright by a passing train. My coachman and I placed the body on a stretcher, covered it, hoisted it upon the seat of the open carriage, and drove homewards. As we slowly traversed the dense crowds of laughing, merry lads and lasses, silence fell as they saw our tragic burden. The impact of sudden death fell on their merrymaking like a heavy hand; faces grew white, laughter was stilled. We drove through the thronged streets, all be-flagged and garlanded, first to the Police Station where the dead man's wife awaited us, then to the mortuary chapel where the uncoffined body was to lie till daybreak. A strange sensation, to ride with death through the surge and tumult of human life, and leave the awed silence of calamity in one's wake.

August 1st. At this moment I am alone in the house (the family, with my brother Peter, minister of Oxnam, having gone to spend this pleasant summer afternoon at Stobo Manse) eagerly awaiting the House of Lords decision in the appeal of the "Wee Free" remnant against the United Free Church. The Court of Session, both in the Outer and Inner Houses, has decided in favour of the U.F. body; but should the "Wee Frees" win to-day, they will retain their churches, manses and endowments intact. Nothing else has been talked of here, and throughout all Scotland, for days; local excitement has risen to fever-heat; it is the one absorbing topic of the moment for every Scottish mind. I have been greatly delayed in my daily rounds, owing to its pre-eminence; controversy has raged so furiously that even chronic complaints have been dethroned in its favour! I now break off to go in search of an evening paper, which should have arrived by now, announcing the fateful decision. . . .

(*Later.*) "The strife is o'er, the battle won"—the "Wee Frees" are victorious! The United Frees are to pay the joint expenses of the appeal; while the "Wee Free" remnant will possess buildings and money valued at some four or five millions. This decision will create a furore throughout Scotland, comparable not so much to a second Reformation as to an ecclesiastical revolution! Some, doubtless, will hope to see the "Wee Frees," with their millions, establish gigantic industrial missions in Africa and India. Others may prophesy a great future reunion by Act of Parliament of all Presbyterian bodies, sharing all endowments, into one united Church of Scotland. Who knows but that this may come one day?

Meanwhile, I have wired the momentous decision to the Manse of Stobo, so that the party there, including as it does two "Auld Kirk" ministers, may be put out of suspense forthwith! Much midnight oil will be burnt in every manse in Scotland, if not in every home, ere all the partisans have said their say on this event to-night.

August 14th. To-night I have completed the unfinished MS. of my brother George's work, *Records of the Baron Court of Stichill*, which he left in the hope that it might ultimately be issued in book form. This I have succeeded in ensuring, through the Scottish Historical Society, which has undertaken to publish the work. I have transcribed the entire MS., adding footnotes, glossary, genealogical tables, appendix and introduction. I am grateful to have been spared to accomplish this task on my brother's behalf, and for the extraordinary way in which, despite all obstacles, a path seems to have been opened up for me from day to day. With this accomplished, I can now resume work on the Presbytery Records. My own transcription of *Peblis to the Play*, too, will shortly appear in book form, and will be dedicated to Winifred—a surprise for her.

May 27th, 1905. To-day I received an unexpected patient—a qualified doctor desiring admission, as an inmate, to the local poorhouse! I bade him sit down, and in a few minutes the brief tale of tragedy was told. He is only forty-five (exactly my own age); drink and drugs have caused his utter ruin. He bears a good Scots name, but has been in practice in England, and has now exhausted the patience and the resources of every available friend. I offered to pay his way to Edinburgh, or to a cottage hospital; he refused, saying, "I have come to the end, and may as well die in the poorhouse as anywhere else." It was the stark truth; I made out the order for admission, and he went. A sorrowful finish to a life still in its prime.

June 25th (Sunday). To-day's sermon was preached by my patient, Professor Charteris, and a fine sermon it was. Strange to see him there in the pulpit, full of energy and eloquence, and to reflect that three years ago he was condemned to death by Treves within two months! His is indeed a case of "Reprieve granted." [1]

[1] Dr Charteris lived three years longer, dying suddenly in 1908 [Ed.].

July 7th. To-night at eight o'clock the fire-bell rang from the church steeple. From the roof of Lindores we observed flames stealing along the western eaves of the Hydropathic, and in a few minutes it became evident that the whole vast structure was threatened, if not doomed. With the children, I hastily cycled to the spot, to find a scene of panic and confusion indescribable. The guests, who had been at dinner when the outbreak was discovered, were now mostly scattered about the lawns, or attempting to save their personal property by raiding the deserted bedrooms while there was yet time to cheat the flames. An old patient of mine, aged eighty-four, in precarious health, lay on the terrace wrapped in blankets; his distracted wife stood by.

We made four rapid journeys to their room, and succeeded in salving all their personal belongings, including various gifts of solid gold which had been presented to them only yesterday—their Golden Wedding anniversary. For hours we toiled back and forth, rescuing property, with crowds of helpers intent on the same mission—also, unknown to us till later, with numerous thieves who, scenting a "haul," had motored out from Edinburgh, and carried off considerable stores of booty!

Meanwhile the flames spread rapidly; about 8.30 the north turret fell with a deafening crash, and an hour later the entire north wing was wrapped in a sheet of fire. Firemen and rescuers alike now realised that the whole huge structure was doomed. Our last and somewhat hazardous raid was in search of a black silk petticoat! The owner, an elderly but pertinacious lady, bombarded us with agitated entreaties and lamentations anent this garment. We ran it to earth at last in a wardrobe, and bore it in triumph through smoke-filled corridors to its owner. From its voluminous recesses she, overjoyed, produced her watch, her purse, all her jewelry, and a wad of bank-notes! Our perseverance was thus rewarded!

When we left the scene, long after midnight, nothing remained of the building save its bare skeleton, still blazing furiously in the darkness and lighting up the countryside for miles around.

October 4th. To-day we witnessed a grim postscript to the great Hydropathic fire which caused such consternation three months ago. Early this morning the ruins were blasted, so that a new building may be permitted to arise, phœnix-like, from the ashes of the old. All went successfully; fifteen pounds of blasting material were employed, with fuses of varying length. After several terrific explosions, the ruined skeleton collapsed like a house of cards, amid the crash of shattered glass and the crumbling of sandstone crushed to powder. Only one accident occurred—a piece of whinstone flew over some adjacent cottages and wounded severely, but not dangerously, a small boy playing in the open.

October 28th. This afternoon I, invited as editor of *Records of the Baron Court of Stichill*, attended the annual meeting of the Scottish Historical Society, with Lord Rosebery in the chair. He spoke in high terms of the book, and of my brother's historical labours and research. When the meeting was over, we had a pleasant talk, and he congratulated me warmly on my share in the work.[1]

[1] Apart from various war-time entries, some of which appear in the following chapter, Dr Gunn's diary ceases at this point. During the intervening years his literary energies appear to have been absorbed in the production of his *Books of the Church* series, the transcription of various vernacular classics, and in racy descriptive letters to his children, one of whom, Jack, was in Malaya [ED.].

1914. Peebles, like every other town, village and
hamlet in the country, is a changed place now-a-days,
shadowed by the black cloud of war. The streets are
quiet as the grave; groups of men stand idle, discuss-
ing the latest news from the Front. The tweed-mills
are closed meanwhile; one misses the tramp of workers
along the pavements, and the sound of the early morning horn.

Arrival of Belgian Refugees. Some thirty refugees—
men, women and children—from Malines, Termonde
and Antwerp, arrived in Peebles on a cold, dreary
October night, and were welcomed by the Provost,
magistrates, ministers, and townspeople. They were
convoyed across the old bridge whose arches had borne
the fleeing feet of fugitives from Flodden Field, four
centuries ago. The night wind fluttered the folds of
their country's flag, borne in advance of the sorrowful
cavalcade. Interpreters in French had been secured,
but alas, the fugitives speak only Flemish, so we could
not converse with them save by means of signs. The
women, many of them with sleeping children in their
arms, appeared worn out, miserable and bewildered.

The parish minister, Dr Martin, like another
Christopher, took one child from its weary mother
and carried it in his arms across the bridge; our
sixteen-year-old Irene followed his example with
another; everyone was eager to help and to befriend
the exiles. But despite the cheering of the welcoming
crowds which lined the streets, it was a sorrowful procession; even the men seemed cowed and dejected,
and all stood in dire need of food and rest. They told

us, in broken phrases, the names of the children—
Marie, Isabeau, Leonard, Ludovic, Thérèse, Baptiste,
and so forth; one white-faced girl was clinging to the
arm of her sweetheart, while another was supported
by two brothers. The whole town seemed, in the
Scriptural phrase, to move about them as they passed
onwards towards shelter, rest and comfort; it was a
profoundly touching and significant sight.

Who could have imagined that we in our day should
witness the dispersal of a nation, recalling in its intimate
features the dispersion of the Jews so many centuries
ago? One recalls, too, Julius Cæsar's dictum, given
half a century before the birth of Christ: *Horum
omnium fortissimi sunt Belgæ* ("Of all the nations (in
Gaul) the Belgians are the bravest"). Had this small
intrepid nation yielded to *force majeure*, as they might
plausibly have done, permitting free passage across
Belgium to the German troops *qui trans Rhenum incolunt,
quibuscum continenter bellum gerunt* ("who live across the
Rhine, and with whom they now continually wage
war"), the course of European destinies might have
been altered. Our Border burgh might have shared
the fate of Malines, of Termonde; and our children
been driven to seek refuge among strangers in a strange
land, like those homeless weary fugitives we welcomed
among us to-night.

A War-time Christmas. Sorrow is everywhere in these
dreary December days, making "the festive season"
a mockery, and "Yuletide greetings" echo grimly in
the ear of death. "Peace on earth, goodwill to men"
—where is it, with this European cataclysm gripping
the nations by the throat—a veritable Armageddon?

To-day—a dreary Sunday morning of snow and
hail—I visited three homes in succession, each the
abode of tragic grief. In the first of these, a newly
made widow was automatically moving to and fro,
preparing breakfast for her two young children.

These, seated by the fire, were gleefully playing with the Field postcards sent from the Front by their father, now lying in a soldier's grave. In the next house, a middle-aged mother sat alone. As I entered, she pointed silently to the table; I took up the telegram which lay there, and read the brief statement of her only son's death—"killed in action"—with the message of sympathy from the King and Lord Kitchener, which accompanied it. Words were useless; I wrung her hand in silence and came away. In the third house sat yet another mother, this time surrounded by kindly sympathising neighbours. The room was lit by a flickering gas-jet, for, though nearly nine o'clock, there was as yet no daylight, only dense December gloom. On the woman's lap lay a few holly leaves from her son's grave, and some shattered fragments of his rifle, which a comrade-in-arms had sent to her. She showed me the accompanying letter; it ended with the words, "I do not know the instant when I myself may be taken; but God has us all in his keeping."

1915. Much of my time is now taken up in examining recruits—fine stalwart country fellows mostly, including many shepherds, gamekeepers and ploughmen. The town is gradually becoming something of a military centre; we wake to the strains of the "Reveillé," and the "Last Post" sounds in our ears at night ere we sleep. On my country journeys in the car, I daily meet battalions of troops returning from manœuvres in the Lyne and Manor valleys or among the Meldon Hills. Trade is now improving somewhat, as the tweed-mills are busy with orders for tartans and khaki for the troops. The adjacent military camps supply our Border lasses with a complete change of sweethearts every few weeks; when one draft leaves for the Front, the "girls they left behind them" are often inconsolable for days. But a fresh contingent arrives, and the gaps are speedily filled up. Thus passes the glory of the world!

A Soldiers' Sacrament Sunday. At an early hour this morning, in the Parish Church, eighty soldiers received the Sacrament at the hands of the minister, Dr Martin, who is also chaplain to the Royal Scots. Not since the days of Cromwell's Ironsides, who worshipped their stern Jehovah with sword in one hand and Bible in the other, has a more significant scene been witnessed in a Border parish. The resonant voices of these bronzed khaki-clad men, singing,

> "Yea, though I walk thro' death's dark vale,
>   Yet will I fear none ill,
>   For Thou art with me, and thy rod
>   And staff me comfort still."

will echo for many a day in many a heart. A great stillness fell upon the assembly as the preacher, himself profoundly stirred, pointed out that many of those present were probably taking the Sacrament for the last time. The ancient oath, or *sacramentum*, of the Roman soldier was visibly re-embodied in that of the Christian. One felt that each of these men was, in a literal sense, dedicated—probably to death, certainly to sacrifice—and that the simple moving solemnity of the Scottish Communion Office was to-day a sacrament in spirit as well as in form.

The battalions of the Royal Scots are, appropriately enough, encamped upon the King's Muir here—the ancient muster-ground of the Burgh forces in time of war, from the fifteenth century onwards. Strange to reflect that on a wooded slope bordering this site, where the trim rows of army tents stand to-day, witches in mediæval times were ruthlessly haled to their doom! The condemned women were convoyed to the stake by ministers of the Presbytery, and the master of ceremonies received from the town, as his official fee, the price of a pair of shoes. On these judicial gala days all the townspeople turned out as to a merry-making; the costs of witch-burnings may still be seen, duly chronicled in the Burgh records. And now, in the twentieth century, when men had hoped that wars, like witch-burnings, were to be no more forever, the old Burgh once again reverts to mediævalism, and bugles echoing night and day disturb the pastoral quiet of the King's Muir.

A great round-up of horses from the adjacent villages and farms took place recently. They were assembled on Tweedgreen for a veterinary inspection, and the selected animals were sent on to the seat of war. Poor beasts, how will they endure the red hell of Flanders, after years spent peacefully ploughing the Border fields? The farmers are now bereft both of men and beasts, and are everywhere turning their land into grass, for lack of labour to cultivate it.

Late one night, returning in the car from a country journey, I came upon some hundreds of soldiers, busily digging trenches for manœuvres on the hill-slopes above Lyne Water. It was a strange scene in that peaceful pastoral valley; row upon row of toiling sweating men, half-concealed within the sandy trenches, throwing out the soil in parapets, while the outspanned wagons stood near by, the tethered horses beside them. As the car approached, the sharp cry of the sentry rang out in the still night: "*Halt! Who goes there?*"

"*Local doctor.*"

"*Pass, local doctor!*"

Onwards we sped, leaving them to their midnight task, while the owls hooted eerily in the darkness, and the merest rim of a waxing moon showed faintly in the starless sky.

1916. To-day (St Patrick's Day, March 17th) we have seen the sun for the first time this year. This winter has been the longest, dreariest and most sunless of any I can remember. The gloom of unlighted streets by night, and of dwellings darkened for fear of air-raids, has added to the universal sorrow and heaviness with which the war-cloud has invested every home in the community.

May 17*th*. Our elder son, George, at present serving as an engineer in H.M.S. ——, has just had two narrow escapes from death, his ship being twice heavily shelled. On the last occasion three men who stood with him in the engine-room were killed, and he himself was wounded. He is certainly compassed about with many and great dangers, but so far has been mercifully preserved.

May 21*st*. The great domestic event of this week, for everyone in the British Isles, has of course been the putting forward of all clocks by Act of Parliament, to inaugurate what is to be known in future as "Summer Time." We performed this unique ceremony at 11 P.M. last night. Henceforward we shall all rise with the lark at 6 A.M., and go to roost with the hens at 9 P.M.! Our staid old Grandfather clock, which has served as a family retainer from one generation to another, and has never within living memory exhibited any signs of caprice, suddenly went out on strike two days before the Act came into force! In vain did I coax and cajole her; soft words and lubricating oil failed equally to affect her stubborn spirit. In the end, we had to dispatch her, still sulking, to the clock doctor for a thorough overhauling. Twelve hours later, inspired by her revolutionary example, my own trusted and hitherto trustworthy watch rebelled in sympathy. So that when the momentous instant finally arrived, both Grandfather and Waltham were absent, and, having recorded their pained protest, duly evaded the legislative insult!

June. Over a hundred German prisoners-of-war— mostly seamen from the *Blücher*, the *Gneisenau* and various submarines—have arrived at Stobo Camp. They are to be employed in timber-felling at Dawyck. Wood for the trenches is in great demand, and trees are being cut down for this purpose all over Scotland, so that in many places the whole face of the country-side is changing from day to day. Huts have been erected to house the prisoners, who in the main look cheerful, healthy and well fed. When summoned in the course of medical duty to attend these men, I advance armed with a revolver, to the gate of a barbed-wire cage, inside which stand the prisoners. An armed sentry unlocks the gate, ushers me in, and locks it behind me. One feels at first like a lion-tamer in a menagerie, but quickly becomes used to the sensation. When at their work in the forest, the men are sur-rounded by armed sentries with fixed bayonets.

The guard has recently been doubled in strength, as well it may be, since it consists for the most part of aged, decrepit, white-haired "dug-outs"—the only men the country can now spare for such a job. Most of these suffer from lumbago and sciatica as well as from Anno Domini; the stalwart German seamen whom they are intended to control, look like giants in the custody of pygmies. The other day I asked one of these venerable veterans his age; he replied "Mili-tary age, sixty; but I'm seventy-nine, Doctor, just the same!" To watch the "Old Guard" shambling and shuffling along in the performance of their official duties is like a Gilbert-and-Sullivan opera.

November. An air-raid warning has just sent us all to crouch, shivering, in the lower regions, with no light except an electric torch, two bicycle lamps, and a solitary candle. It is a wearing business, waiting in suspense for the possible bomb to annihilate the family circle. We beguiled the weary moments by trying to decide what it would be most impressive to be found holding when the Call came. Lord Tennyson, we

remembered, in a perilous predicament, held a copy of
Cymbeline! Various suggestions were made, including
The Christian Herald, Burns's Works, *Punch*, *The British
Weekly*, and, of course, the Bible. *A Doctor's Thoughts*
was also debated, but alas, found only one supporter!
In the end we unanimously decided on cats—the mother-
cat for the head of the family, and a kitten apiece for
each member of the household. Our Call has, however, been meanwhile providentially postponed.

1917. The war is now bearing very hardly on
doctors whose age unfits them for medical service
abroad. Conditions at home are very complex;
many doctors left their practices at the outset in charge
of junior men, hoping to find some remnants at least
on their return. These deputies are now being called
up in their turn, and the practices scattered to the four
winds. It is now impossible to secure any kind of
locum tenens, male or female. I have had to abandon
all literary effort meanwhile, and am fatigued with the
pressure of additional unaccustomed work—yet, like
every other doctor, must e'en thole as best I can. The
local War Hospital, of which I am in charge, absorbs
much time and energy. But it goes well, and the
patience and courage of the wounded men more than
repay any efforts on their behalf. I have just had the
satisfaction, too, of receiving a tabulated statement of
subsistence costs for all Scottish war hospitals, and of
finding that ours are the lowest ($8\frac{1}{2}$d. per day per head).
Yet the weight-charts show that our patients are the
heaviest and healthiest in the whole area.

Food questions now form an acute problem of daily
life. Proclamations anent Food Economy are read
from time to time from the Church pulpit during
service-time. These strange-sounding additions to the
rubric exhort us to abjure, not as of yore the seven
deadly sins, but the scarce wheaten loaf and scarcer
joint of meat, and to cleave, instead, to oatmeal

porridge and the still plentiful potato. Meanwhile a communal kitchen has been opened in one of the tweed-mills, where, for eightpence, the employees can dine daily.

Butter is almost unprocurable, even at 3s. 4d. per pound; eggs are 4d. each; coals are both dear and scanty; petrol stands at 4s. 3d. per gallon, and is of very poor quality at that. Sugar is so scarce that I have had to resort to subterfuge in order to replenish my private bowl, containing the weekly ration, which I find indispensable to my system. A patient having presented me with a pound (more to be desired than gold) I rose each morning early and stealthily increased the microscopic quantity lurking at the foot of the bowl; all went well until one day Irene, her own ration exhausted, perceived with envy and amazement that mine continued almost unimpaired! I bade her read the Bible and, like the widow with her cruse, have faith, as I had; but was informed that the modern Elisha had been detected nefariously adding his pickle of meal to the girnel and his drop of oil to the cruse!

The other day we attended a wedding—an unusual dissipation in war-time, when such affairs are generally hurried through without ceremony or celebrations. As at present no one, save war profiteers, spends a penny on dress if it can be by any means avoided, our respective "wedding garments" gave rise to much earnest cogitation. My wife, in her "party best" (purple charmeuse gown, Beefeater hat and feather boa to match), was, as I informed her, an easy first in the Married Ladies' Class; Irene, who is at present acting as my chauffeuse, wore her attractive uniform. I myself donned an aged frock-coat, with trousers also long past their prime, a new lavender tie, and a venerable silk hat, *ætat* twelve years at least—the *tout ensemble* admirably representing an ultra-dignified country doctor of the last century! No sooner had the knot been tied than I was urgently summoned to the country; so we hastily shed our wedding apparel, and my young chauffeuse resumed her post at the wheel. So far she gives her employer every satisfaction; keeps the car lamps and brasses gleaming like molten gold; and has the lightest touch of any driver I have ever had. An old friend who was also among the wedding-guests told me an anecdote worth recording. The County Buildings of our Royal Burgh were designed by the eminent Edinburgh architect, Bryce, who one day summoned a Peebles plasterer, Dawson Brown, to his office in the city, with a view to ascertaining his fitness to undertake some plaster-work in arabesque, with which it was proposed to adorn the ceilings. The great architect opened the interview by remarking caustically, "Of course, you can't be expected to do anything worth while, any of you, out there in Peebles!" Silence reigned after this unpromising prelude; Brown moved towards the office window, where he stood mute, wrapt in steadfast contemplation of the adjacent Scott Monument in Princes Street.

"What are you looking at, man?" inquired Bryce at length, impatiently.

"Juist that Monument there, that was designed by yin o' oor puir Peeblesshire lads, that spent his time maistly makin' dung-barrows!"

The "puir Peeblesshire lad" was George Meikle Kemp, the country joiner who achieved fame as the architect of the Scott Monument. Brown's bow, drawn at a venture, found its mark; Bryce there and then appointed him to undertake the job, and his good workmanship survives in the County Buildings to this day.

Once a week, as Medical Officer, I continue to visit the Prisoners' Camp at Stobo, where I usually have to examine about a score of prisoners and at least a dozen members of the veteran guard. I am also responsible for all operations which have to be performed; and am obliged to furnish detailed weekly reports in addition. Each visit involves a special journey of fifteen miles; yet the official remuneration is 10s. per visit! Recently, while my own car was temporarily disabled, I had to hire one for these visits at 15s. per journey, which left me not only minus profit, but out of pocket. At long last I have resolved to apply to the Senior Medical Officer at Edinburgh Castle, in the hope that something may be done to improve this state of affairs.

On one of my recent visits, four of the prisoners complained of severe foot-trouble, and begged me to allow them to exchange their wooden clogs for leather boots. As after careful examination I could detect nothing amiss with their feet, I refused this request. The sequel justified both my diagnosis and my caution. Two days later, these four foot-sufferers, while engaged in their usual task of timber-felling, eluded the guard and made good their escape into the forest. For a fortnight they succeeded in evading pursuit, living meanwhile on potatoes, corn and turnips (whether begged, borrowed or stolen, did not transpire). Finally they were recaptured, and brought back to the camp. I was summoned to examine them on their return, and found them dirty, unshaven and badly scratched from barbed-wire, but otherwise none the worse for their adventure. They displayed with some pride the treasure-trove they had collected—chocolate, matches, various food-stuffs, a large frying-pan, and over 800 cigarettes! All these of course were confiscated, and each runaway sentenced to fourteen days' solitary confinement.

1918. This sorrowful war still drags on. We at home are weary, discouraged, and sick at heart; what then must it be for those who are bearing the burden and heat of the day at the Front?

All through these dreary years I have made it a

habit whenever possible to stand bareheaded at the gate of this house whenever a company of soldiers passes, and to salute them as they go. One evening lately, close on midnight, I watched a battalion march past, returning from their long day's labour in the open. They were young lads for the most part; footsore, dog-tired, and dumb—too weary even to sing. Silently they passed between the rows of sleeping houses, along the lampless streets, making for the haven of their tents and the brief respite of a few hours' sleep. As I stood silently in salute, the idea came to me that the heroism and sacrifice of our Border lads—tailors, clerks, printers, mechanics, officers and privates alike —should somehow be commemorated for all time, in an enduring form. Why not a commemorative volume for the Burgh of Peebles—or better still, for the whole County? One could compile a brief record of each man who has laid down his life, with a short summary of his career, and perhaps a photograph inset.

I have resolved to undertake a Book of Remembrance on these lines, and shall make a start with the work without delay. In this way, however inadequately, one can at least chronicle the deeds, and honour the memory, of the unreturning brave.

March 1st. To-day Manor Valley Sanatorium, of which I have for many years been Medical Officer, and which I visit thrice weekly, proved all but unapproachable owing to the effects of a tremendous blizzard of snow and wind which has been raging for some days. The building stands in an isolated position on a hill-slope high above Manor Valley, and exposed to all the winds of heaven. The car was of course useless in the deep snow; I had to use a carriage and two horses as far as Manor Church, then take to the fields on foot and struggle as best I could up the slopes to the Sanatorium. All the shelters, many of them filled with tubercular patients desperately ill, were buried deep in drifted snow; fallen chimneys and broken glass lay all around; the telephone wires were down; the havoc wrought by the hurricane was greatly aggravated by the piled-up masses of frozen snow, and by the intense piercing cold. But for the resourceful courageous spirit of the matron, Miss Paton, hospital work under such circumstances would be a hopeless task; but she brings to these Crimean conditions the spirit of Florence Nightingale.

For some time the prisoners at Stobo Camp have been in a state of grave mental unrest, due partly to low rations, home-sickness, and the ennui of confinement; partly also to the news of German military reverses, which depresses and inflames them by turns. I have had to visit the camp daily for over a week, to examine batches of men declaring themselves unfit for duty. Most of their complaints prove, on investigation, to have no basis in fact; I then have to order them back to work, or if they refuse, to the solitary cells, at the mouth of a revolver. Now, however, discontent and hysteria have culminated in anarchy; half the prisoners have been escorted to Edinburgh in charge of a military patrol, there to be punished for mutiny, and those who remain behind appear to be heading for the same fate.

October–November. As though war conditions had not brought sorrow enough, with maimed men daily patrolling our streets, every hospital overflowing with wounded, and shell-shock cases crowding the mental wards, the worst influenza epidemic in my remembrance is now upon us. Schools are closed; business at a standstill; churches half-empty; the hearse seldom idle. In less than three weeks there have been over thirty deaths in this small community. Septic double pneumonia accounts for most of these, the principal victims being young mothers and infants. We doctors have had an exhausting battle, working day and night; yet the plague is not stayed. Daily, at present, I visit from sixty to seventy homes, each containing from three to nine patients, all suffering from the disease. This hard unremitting work alone is enough to exhaust one; but the anxiety, suspense, responsibility, disappointment and sorrow which such an epidemic entails, weigh down the heart like a millstone.

November 11th. Signing of the Armistice.

No man who has lived to see this day will ever forget it—a day of joy too deep for mere rejoicings, of pride and sorrow too profound for expression, of thankfulness which far transcends words. "The war is over —peace has come—now thank we all our God"; such are the words that echo in every heart. Here, as everywhere, emotion has found vent in much clanging of bells, waving of flags, screaming of horns, and so forth. Banners and streamers flutter everywhere; every house has blossomed into bunting; our staid Border folk sing and dance in the streets. I visited the German prisoners' camp; found the men thankful and happy at the prospect of peace at any price, eagerly making plans for their return to homes and kindred.

At night I worked for an hour or two on my projected Book of Remembrance for the fallen. Then to Church, with the entire household, to share in a joint service of thanksgiving, in which all religious bodies took part. So we write "Finis" to the long blood-stained chapter of war, and turn the page. In the end, "he that tholes, overcomes"—those who died, and we who live, are to-day united in spirit as never before; their victory is our inspiration, their sacrifice our incentive to a better life.

CHAPTER XI

OUTWARD BOUND—THE LAST
CARGO—A FRIEND'S SALUTE—
JOURNEY'S END

DURING the years immediately following the war the doctor devoted his scanty leisure to the completion of a unique and intensely laborious task. The idea of a Book of Remembrance, which he conceived on that spring evening in 1918 while saluting a battalion of Borderers on the march, expanded into a massive compilation in five volumes, which was only completed in 1925. Seven years of arduous, ungrudging toil were devoted to this task. As a result, the *Books of Remembrance for Peebles, West Linton and Tweeddale* present an authentic commemorative record, with portrait, of every man connected with the county of Peeblesshire who laid down his life in the war.[1]

In recognition of this immense work the doctor received in 1922 the highest honour in the gift of the community—the Freedom of the Royal Burgh of Peebles, when it was conferred simultaneously on Field-Marshal Earl Haig.

These post-war years saw also the completion of the doctor's Presbyterial records of the Church in every parish of Peeblesshire. Through this herculean task, which for some thirty years had absorbed a great part of his leisure, he amassed for future historians a wealth of ecclesiastical and social data upon which to draw at will. Scottish civic conditions and domestic manners, no less than purely parochial events, are

[1] On a pillar in Peebles Parish Church, a bronze tablet above the doctor's seat now bears the inscription: "Here was wont to sit Clement Bryce Gunn, M.D., Historian of the Churches of Tweeddale, and Chronicler of the unreturning brave [1914–1918]." [ED.]

illuminated in these fourteen volumes by countless vivid and often entertaining sidelights, which the student of national history may well acknowledge with gratitude.[1]

Yet another activity, pursued with tireless undiscouraged energy during these difficult years, was the doctor's long-cherished scheme for the restoration and preservation of the ruined Cross Kirk of Peebles. Eventually, largely owing to his indomitable efforts, H.M. Office of Works undertook and completed this task. The former "abomination of desolation" was converted into a spacious grass-clad demesne; all traces of neglect and vandalism were blotted out, and the historic sanctuary, duly scheduled as an "Ancient Monument," now ranks among the beauty spots of the old Border burgh.

A religious service instituted and conducted by the doctor was annually held in its precincts. Often, too, a casual stranger, skirting the cloister-garth which borders the ruins, would be arrested by the echo of youthful laughter and the sight of a great concourse of eager children, with the doctor's upright, grey-clad figure in their midst. Always his merry jest or unexpected twist of phrase would kindle the upturned faces into quick response, as he linked the good St Nicholas, once venerated at this same shrine, with the familiar Santa Claus to whom every child pays hopeful tribute on Christmas Eve.[2]

Unabated and manifold energies such as these left

[1] The few Church histories left completed but unpublished by Dr Gunn are now preserved in the Scottish National Library, Edinburgh, and may be consulted there [ED.].

[2] Eighteen months after Dr Gunn's death, public gratitude for his labours on behalf of the Cross Kirk was commemorated by a tablet set up within its restored precincts. This was unveiled (16th June 1935) by his widow, when Principal Cairns (Aberdeen), in presence of a great assemblage, delivered a moving and memorable oration [ED.].

the mind little margin, even in latter years, for rest or recreation. But the shortening day was often cheered and brightened by the pleasure of companionship with his three grandchildren. To one of these, Cameron Rusby, he and his wife acted for some time *in loco parentis*, in the absence of their daughter, Irene, with her husband, an officer in the Royal Navy then serving abroad.

The last few years of the doctor's life (already saddened by the loss of his two brothers, Tom, the advocate, and Peter, the minister of Oxnam) were harassed by much physical suffering. This he "tholed" in characteristic and courageous silence. Though his vital energies were slowly, almost imperceptibly, weakening under stress of ill-health, his gallant spirit would brook no curtailment of his professional tasks. He was one of those who "consume their own smoke with an extra draught of hard work."

To die in harness had always been his ambition; it was fulfilled. To the last he visited his patients, going in and out among them with alert step and stimulating presence, always with a jest on his lips, and the warmth of human kindness in his firm handclasp. So gallantly did he keep the flag flying, that no one could have guessed that the ship was nearing the end of the voyage, with the tide "too full for sound or foam" already at the turn.

Early one November morning in 1933 a few chance spectators watched the doctor, with his wife, leave the house he had built and lived in for nearly forty years, step into a waiting car, and drive quietly away to an Edinburgh nursing home, as though setting out on an ordinary country journey. During the weeks which followed, that serene fearlessness with which he had faced blizzard and tempest, flooded river and daunting snowdrift for so many arduous years of country practice, carried him undefeated through the last and longest journey. The devoted surgeon and nurses, with the friends who visited him, all acknowledged with amazement his unconquerable vitality of mind and spirit.

To his minister and friend, the Rev. Berry Preston, as he lay dying, he summed up his lifelong creed in three words: "*Laborare est orare.*" Another friend who shared the last hours (Rev. John Cruickshank) thus epitomised the doctor's devotion to his calling: "To Clement Gunn, his profession was a religion."

On Christmas morning (a few days after his seventy-third birthday), as the church bells of his beloved native city of Edinburgh rang out their joyous message, the end came in complete tranquillity of spirit.

Late that Christmas night there swept past the historic cross of the old Border town, where in every home that day the shadow of mourning had lain heavy on men's hearts, a silent, swift-moving car. It bore the doctor's body, clad by his own wish in his customary everyday suit of grey. Close behind came another car, driven by his elder son, who had thus borne him company through the dark miles of a midnight journey for the last time. Down the deserted street they passed towards the church, where at the top of the high flight of steps a small sorrowing group awaited them, and light poured through the open doorway in readiness for the doctor's homecoming. As the coffin was carried within, a casual spectator, passing by, saw a brilliant meteor flash suddenly across the midnight sky, and vanish in the dark immensities of space. So aptly symbolic did that transit appear to the watcher that he recorded it later in the public Press.

In his study, a stone's-throw from the church where the doctor's body lay, his familiar friend, Walter Buchan, sat pen in hand. His words do more than salute the friend; they etch the man, clear-cut, "in his habit as he lived." He wrote:—

" *The Interpreter then called for a man-servant of his, one Great-Heart.*"—BUNYAN's *Pilgrim's Progress*.

"*In every age, in every generation, there are a few—sometimes very few—who, by their ability, energy, enthusiasm, and large-hearted charity, impress their contemporaries and invigorate the life of the community in which they live. Such a man was Clement Bryce Gunn. Those who were fortunate enough to be his friends valued his friendship as something precious, which they knew it would not be possible to replace. He is dead, and it seems as if a brightness had gone from the air.*

"'*I never think of Peebles without thinking of Dr Gunn!*' '*The town without him will never be the same.*' *These are statements which have been made, and they contain an essence of truth, for no one—in this generation at least—had made himself so integral a part of Peebles. It was a fortunate chance that brought Dr Gunn to this Border town almost half-a-century ago. His attractive personality at once made itself felt, and for many years his influence has been an ever-growing one.*

"*He became identified with the inner life of many of the homes in the town and district. Patients he had of every class, and for all he did his best, fighting the unceasing illnesses that flesh is heir to; but it was to the poor and the unfortunate that he gave his heart. To them he was not only a doctor, but a friend who upheld them amid the troubles of life. Very often when sustaining food was required and funds were scarce, it was the Doctor who provided the necessary nourishment—at his own expense. His name and memory will be long cherished. He loved his fellow-men, and thought nobly of the soul.*

"*He often saw human nature at its worst, but always he had an understanding sympathy and something of the large generosity of Falstaff when he defended, with warm geniality, his ragged band against the outspoken criticisms of Prince Hal:—'Tush, man—mortal men, mortal men.'*

> '*He took such cognizance of men and things,*
> *If any beat a horse you felt he saw;*
> *If any cursed a woman, he took note;*
> *Yet stared at nobody—you stared at him,*
> *And found, less to your pleasure than surprise,*
> *He seemed to know you and expect as much.*
> *So, next time that a neighbour's tongue was loosed,*

193

It marked the shameful and notorious fact :
We had among us not so much a spy,
As a recording chief inquisitor—
The town's true master, if the town but knew.'

"He never spared himself if there was anything he could do to help. His life had no narrow selfish boundaries, and even at the last he thought not of himself, but of others. It was typical of him that he should continue his work till the very end, without murmur or complaint, even when suffering pain and discomfort, and conscious that his body was failing him.

"Amid all his work he remained light-hearted, and, in spite of the discipline of life, he carried with him to the end the eager enthusiasm of a boy. Born and bred a Victorian, he cherished old manners, customs, and settled modes of thought. But he had also respect for the changed points of view of a restless post-war generation, though occasionally his blue eyes wore a puzzled look.

"His conversation sparkled with sudden quips and jests, and there are many in Peebles who delight to tell stories to show forth his quick wit. He was a master of the unexpected retort to an ordinary conventional remark. . . . His mind was quick, and he abhorred idleness.

"He was a poet, too, in odd moments, and played with his thoughts in a delicate fancy, but he was never an introspective moralist. There was something of the Shorter Catechist in his nature, but there was also 'a dash of Puck, a streak of Ariel.'

"He had a passionate love of Scotland, of the Borders in particular, and of Peebles in the last degree. And he loved— as Scott loved, and as Stevenson loved—the people of the country against the background of their national history and traditions. That was why he probed deeply into the history of Peebles. Always it was the past that fired his imagination and made him spend laborious but delightful hours in compiling the records of the churches, and in telling and re-telling the story of Neidpath Castle and of the Cross Kirk.

"His life was a happy one, for he was happy in his professional work, happy in his literary work, and, best of all, happy in his home.

"He coveted no honours for himself; the satisfaction of work well done was to him its own reward. But for his friends, and those near and dear to him, he desired much. It was a great joy

194

to him when his daughter's fine play, Scott of Abbotsford, *was so successfully produced in Glasgow. The first night will always be a pleasant memory. He sat in the stage-box, and his face glowed with pride and happiness; his wife was with him, and together they witnessed their daughter's triumph. All his friends rejoiced with him that night.*

"*As these words are being written, the town is quiet, and the streets are deserted. It is night. And in the old Parish Church, the history of which he knew so well, Great-Heart is lying. He has gone from us, carrying with him a rich harvest of garnered affection and enduring love; and there are many in Peebles who are sore at heart, grieving that they will see him no more, and that they must continue life's journey without him.*

> '*For those who must journey*
> *Henceforward alone*
> *Have need of stout convoy*
> *Now Great-Heart is gone. . . .*' "

Two days later, to the exultant surge of the *Hallelujah Chorus* (his own choice), the doctor's body was borne from the church door on a farm cart garlanded with holly, through streets thronged with weeping crowds, to lie among the graves of Border folk close to the Border hills he had so long known and loved. The long procession, headed by Provost and Magistrates in robes of office, wound its way up the steep hill so often traversed by his own faithful step, while the mournful tolling of the town bell echoed in the wintry air. As the farm cart with its burden drew level with the doctor's own door, with the familiar brass plate gleaming at the gateway, the lines he had written many years earlier of that same home which he had built, found their fulfilment:—

"And one day smoke will rise, and windows in the morn
    Grow bright, though pass the Founder to the tryst
    Which all must keep:—God grant his soul meet Christ!"